GREAT CENTERS
OF PRO BASKETBALL

Action-packed profiles of basketball's big men:
Bob Lanier, Dave Cowens,
Swen Nater, Bob McAdoo,
and Wes Unseld.

GREAT CENTERS
OF PRO BASKETBALL

BY BOB RUBIN

illustrated with photographs

RANDOM HOUSE · NEW YORK

PHOTOGRAPH CREDITS: Vernon J. Biever, 6, 68; Doug Bruce (Camera 5), 51; Malcolm W. Emmons, 2, 6–7, 37, 78, 94, 126, 136, 141; United Press International, 11, 12, 19, 23, 27, 32, 54, 59, 61, 66, 86, 89, 103, 113, 115, 118, 121, 131, 145; Virginia Squires, 109; Wide World Photos, endpapers, 4, 39, 45, 73, 83, 92, 99, 148.
Cover photo by John D. Hanlon (Sports Illustrated).

Copyright © 1975 by Random House, Inc.
All rights reserved under International and Pan-American Copyright Conventions. Published in the United States by Random House, Inc., New York, and simultaneously in Canada by Random House of Canada Limited, Toronto.

Library of Congress Cataloging in Publication Data
Rubin, Bob.   Great centers of pro basketball.   (Pro basketball library)
SUMMARY: Biographical sketches of professional basketball stars include Bob Lanier, Dave Cowens, Bob McAdoo, Swen Nater, and Wes Unseld.
1. Basketball—Biography—Juvenile literature. [1. Basketball—Biography] I. Title.
GV884.AIR8   796.32'3'0922 [B]   [920]   75-8078
ISBN 0-394-83134-9   ISBN 0-394-93134-3 (lib. bdg.)

Manufactured in the United States of America   1 2 3 4 5 6 7 8 9 0

To
Sam
and **Ali,**
the sunshine
of
my life

Contents

Bob Lanier	*8*
Dave Cowens	*36*
Bob McAdoo	*68*
Swen Nater	*94*
Wes Unseld	*118*
Index	*149*

"The fans will never get to know me as a man, so all I can offer them is myself as a player."

Bob Lanier

"Lanier, you're a bum!"
"Hey, fat man!"
"Thar she blows!"
"They oughta paint 'Goodyear' on his side!"
"The Pistons paid a million bucks for *him*?"

Cobo Arena in Detroit, Michigan, rang with boos and catcalls. Thousands of frustrated Piston fans jeered as rookie center Bob Lanier waddled up and down the court in a vain effort to keep up with speedy Dave Cowens of the Boston Celtics. Although the 1970–71 season had just begun, most of the fans had already made up their minds about the young giant their team had signed to a whopping $1.3 million, five-year contract. Their verdict: thumbs down.

In truth, the 6-foot-11 Lanier hardly looked like a million-dollar ballplayer. He weighed close to 290 pounds, and much of the weight was hanging in rolls around his ample middle. He was in obviously poor condition. Every few minutes he had to leave the game to catch his breath. The effort it took simply to run up and down the court showed plainly on his face.

Lanier was suffering from more than just a weight problem, though. He was playing in pain. His right knee, which had undergone major surgery seven months earlier, still ached when he subjected it to the stress of playing basketball.

The truth is that he was overweight and out of condition because his mending knee had prevented him from working out the summer before the start of his first pro season. And even a healthy rookie deserved more time before being judged a flop. But there he was, inexperienced, overweight, in pain, and limping to a chorus of boos as he tried to hold his own in the world's toughest league.

Some rookies might have cracked under such extreme pressure, or at least sounded off in anger. Lanier simply endured it all in silence, even though the criticism was basically unfair. His problems were not of his own making. Lanier made a vow to himself: Someday his critics would eat their words.

Four years later the fans at Cobo Arena were as vocal as ever. But now they were cheering the man

An inexperienced rookie in 1970, Bob Lanier (16) doesn't seem to know quite what to do with the ball . . .

. . . but four years later, the Piston superstar drives to the basket with total assurance.

they had once booed. The Pistons had just defeated the Buffalo Braves, thanks largely to Bob Lanier's 36 points, 22 rebounds, and countless intimidating defensive moves.

"Moses, Moses, Moses!" chanted Piston forward Curtis Rowe, flinging his arms toward the ceiling in mock worship of the grinning Lanier.

"Our man Moses," echoed All-Pro guard Dave Bing.

"Our leader!" shouted another Piston.

"Our healer!" added another.

"Listen to those guys, will you?" said Lanier in mock annoyance. "They think I'm Moses."

"Why don't you part the Detroit River and shut them up?" one reporter suggested.

"I just might do that," Lanier replied.

Even Lanier couldn't part the Detroit River, but in the eyes of the Pistons and their followers there was little else he couldn't do. A sleek (for him) 260 pounds, Lanier had become one of the best big men in pro basketball, a dominating force who could destroy an opponent with his shooting, defense, and rebounding.

Outside the locker room, happy Piston fans dispersed slowly, still singing the praises of big Bob Lanier. In the last four years, Lanier had given them plenty to cheer about. The year before he joined the team, Detroit had finished in last place in the NBA's Eastern Division with a 31–51 record. Four years later, with a mature, healthy giant in the pivot, they turned in a 52–30 record, the best mark in the club's 26-year history. They also made the post-season playoffs for the first time in six years.

Lanier's individual contributions to Detroit's success were considerable. A graceful, accurate, left-handed shooter with an amazing range for a man of his size, Lanier utilized a one-handed jump shot and a soft, sweeping hook as his main offensive weapons. After scoring 15.6 points per game as a part-time starter in his rookie season, Lanier went on to average 25.7, 23.8, 22.5 and 24.0 in his next four years. He maintained an impressive degree of accuracy, sinking 51 percent of his attempts during his first five professional seasons.

Lanier was just as effective under the boards. Using his great bulk to box out opponents under the basket, he averaged 14.2, 14.9, 13.3, and 12.0 rebounds per game after his disappointing rookie season. It took him a little longer to master the difficult art of playing top defense, which is true of almost all beginning pros. But eventually Lanier mastered that vital aspect of the game, too. Here again, his 260 pounds came in handy, enabling him to lean on opponents and force them to shoot from further out than they'd like. When Bob Lanier leaned on someone, he made his presence felt.

Lanier's vow to show his critics that he was worth every cent he received had long since been fulfilled.

The fans who had ridiculed the stumbling, bumbling, bloated rookie never dreamed he'd progress so far so fast, but Lanier never had any doubts. He had been taunted before and wound up getting the last laugh.

Born in Buffalo, New York, in 1948, Lanier was a big baby who just grew and grew. "At five years of age, Bob looked twelve," his father recalled. By the time Bob was twelve, he stood 6-foot-2 and wore a size eleven shoe. His parents were too poor to always keep him in shoes that fit. His grammar school teacher recalled having to call Mr. Lanier to school just once—when Bob picked up a much smaller classmate and threw him across the room for hiding one of his huge sneakers.

Like many big boys, Lanier's growth outstripped his coordination. His size and clumsiness made him the butt of jokes by smaller, more agile boys. And like many big boys who become the butt of jokes, he became shy and withdrawn.

Fortunately, Lanier came to the attention of Lonnie Alexander, the athletic director of the Buffalo Boys Club. "When Bob first came in at age eleven, I noticed how tall he was for his age," said Alexander. "I asked him if he played basketball, and he said no. I asked why not, and he said his elementary school coach said he was too awkward."

That coach may have been cruel to be so blunt with a sensitive young boy, but his judgment of

Bob's athletic abilities was accurate. "Bob had to be taught to run without falling," recalled Alexander. Because Lanier was so self-conscious, Alexander permitted him to work out after the club had closed so he could avoid the ridicule of other boys. "It took over two years before he stopped making mistakes," Alexander said. "Even after he was in high school, I still had him play for the Boys Club. I didn't want him to get down on himself. As he grew, his confidence grew. In his junior year, when he was about six-foot-five, we let him play in high school."

Lanier's coordination improved under Alexander and so did his confidence. By the time Bob was in high school, he was not only a good basketball player but also a star pitcher in the Police Athletic League and a local table tennis champion. But there was one thing he still lacked—aggressiveness.

"I remember one basketball game," said Alexander, "when we were playing Humboldt YMCA for the championship. They were just hitting him and pushing him around without Bob doing anything to protect himself. I told him, 'You gotta get rough. You can't let yourself get mauled.' He went out and knocked down several of the other boys. From then on, nobody took advantage of him."

Playing varsity basketball for Bennett High School in his junior and senior years, Lanier led his team to two Buffalo city championships. He became Buffalo's all-time high school scoring leader, made the All-State team, and received more than a hundred scholarship offers. A home boy, Lanier chose nearby St. Bonaventure. "I wanted to play where my parents could come and see me play," he explained. "I never wanted to be too far away from my mother's cooking, either."

Bigger, stronger, and far more sure of himself, Lanier was a major force in college basketball. He averaged 26.2 points per game as a sophomore, 27.2 as a junior, and 29.1 as a senior. His career field-goal percentage was a sparkling 57.5, and he set school records for total points (2,067) and rebounds (1,180).

The highlight of his years at St. Bonaventure came against Purdue in the championship game of New York's 1970 Holiday Festival. In front of a packed house in Madison Square Garden Lanier poured in 50 points to lead his team to an easy victory. "Lanier is tremendous," said Purdue coach George King. "His agility is amazing, and he has a fabulous shooting touch."

The Lanier who awed King and almost every other opponent in no way resembled the clumsy boy who had once practiced alone in the Buffalo Boys Club gym, with one exception—no, two exceptions —his feet. They were still huge, and people still made fun of them.

Lanier wore specially built size 22 sneakers, which the people at Converse say are the biggest they've ever made. Bob once visited the Seneca Indian reservation near St. Bonaventure and earned the nickname "Ha-You-Non-Da," which means "He Leaves Tracks." People would look at Lanier's feet and ask, "When's the launching?" Once, after a game between St. Bonaventure and Temple, Philadelphia sportswriter Bill Conlin wrote, "At 8:40, Bob Lanier's feet began to emerge from the St. Bonaventure locker room. At 8:45, Bob Lanier emerged."

Lanier didn't mind all the jokes about his feet, but he wanted to make sure people knew that there was more to Bob Lanier than just a pair of gunboats for sneakers.

"It bugs me the way a newscaster can say something about my feet and nothing about the talent I have," he once said. "It would be okay if I was a clumsy ox. But I'm not. Maybe my feet have something to do with my ability. But I really don't mind that much. It's made a lot of people notice me, and I've gotten a lot of publicity out of it."

Unfortunately, Bob's feet also caused him a lot of pain and heartbreak. In 1970, Chris Ford of Villanova (who went on to become one of Lanier's Piston teammates) tripped over one of Bob's giant feet in a post-season NCAA tournament and fell across his legs. The great St. Bonaventure senior writhed on the floor in agony, the inside of his right knee badly torn. The injury marked a tragic end to Lanier's

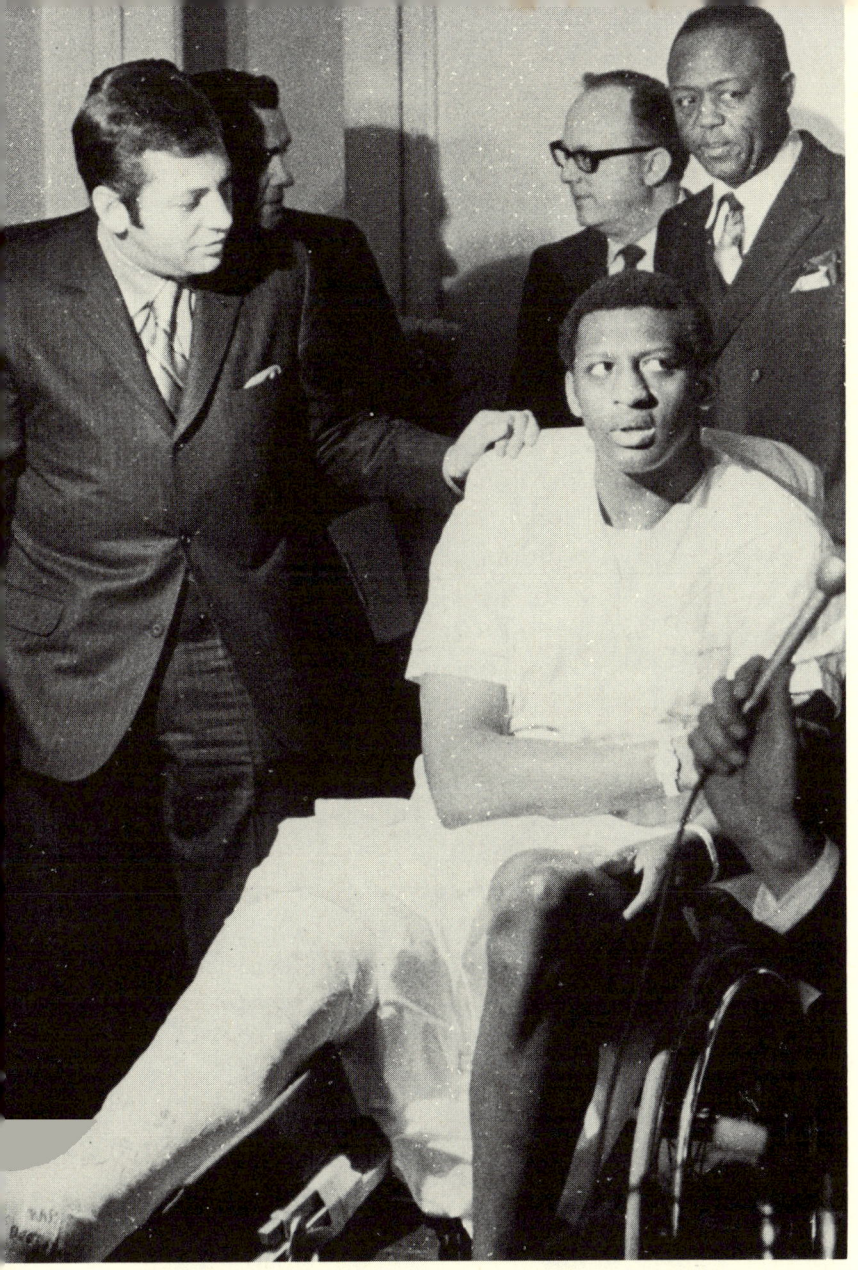

After signing with Detroit in 1970, a badly injured Lanier speaks to newsmen while his agent (left) and father (right) look on.

magnificent college career and turned the early months of his professional career into a time of trial.

The Pistons, who had outbid the ABA's New York Nets for Lanier, were shocked on the first day of training camp when they saw what they had bought for $1.3 million. Lanier limped around the court like a wounded hippo. He was fat and puffing. His knee bore an ugly, zipper-like scar.

One day early in camp, Lanier tripped over rookie guard Harvey Marlatt. As Bob crashed to the floor, his horrified teammates heard loud popping noises coming from the big rookie's sore right knee. Everyone held his breath, fearful that more damage had been done. But fortunately for Lanier, the popping was only the sound of adhesions breaking. (Adhesions are made up of scar tissue that forms after surgery. They act as a protective layer while a wound is healing but eventually must be broken for full mobility to return.)

"Bob broke them all in one day," said Piston coach Butch Van Breda Kolff, searching desperately for a ray of sunshine in a dismal situation. "The doctor said he'll be better off in the long run. So that fall turned out to be a blessing in disguise."

It didn't seem like much of a blessing to Lanier, however. The 1970–71 season began, and he was forced to share the pivot with journeyman Otto Moore. Lanier simply wasn't up to playing a full game. Their high hopes dashed, the Piston fans turned on the high-priced rookie with a vengeance.

"I knew what they were saying about me in the beginning, calling me the Million Dollar Bum," Lanier said. "But you go back and look at the movies. Study them. I had no lateral movement in my legs. I couldn't get off my hook shot and I couldn't move from side to side at all. I'm not a good jumper. I've got to move laterally to get into position to shoot. I just couldn't do it. . . . It was a bad situation."

Throughout that miserable season Lanier maintained his hope and belief that things would change. And they did. His knee gradually got better, he lost weight, and his agility, mobility, and endurance improved. By the end of his rookie year, he was the starting Detroit center. His self-confidence soared. He had turned the corner.

By his second season, Lanier was once more displaying the delicate scoring touch that had made him a college standout. But he still was not the dominant force he could have been. That would take more time and seasoning.

For one thing, critics said he shot from too far out. Even though he did manage to make a good percentage of his long jump shots, it didn't take a basketball genius to see that he would make an even higher percentage shooting from 10 feet out instead of 20. And, of course, there is no better percentage shot in basketball than a dunk.

Lanier had nothing against the short-range shot—he just couldn't get into position for it. He would set up in the low post, but his defender would shove him out a little. He'd set up again—and get shoved out a little more. By the time someone threw him a pass, he'd be 20 feet away from the basket. And as one teammate put it: "Guys who are six-foot-eleven and two hundred and eighty pounds don't win games for you by hitting twenty-foot jump shots."

A far more significant weakness in Lanier's game was his defense. During his brief career as a television commentator during the 1971–72 season, ex-Celtic Bill Russell, whose inspired defense had once led Boston to eleven championships in thirteen seasons, offered a scathing but accurate appraisal of Lanier's defensive ability. The Pistons took note of Russell's blast and decided to do something about it. When the season ended, they hired Russell to teach Lanier the tricks of the trade.

To Lanier's credit, he welcomed help from the man who had publicly blasted him. "I remember how he greeted me," Lanier recalled, laughing. "He said, 'You big overweight ox, I'm gonna run that baby fat off you.' He wasn't kidding, either. Run, run, run all the time. He had no mercy. I lost fifteen pounds, going from two hundred and eighty to two sixty-five."

Lanier also learned how and when to leave his man to harass an opponent attempting to drive for a

To hit his long-range jumper, Lanier has to shoot over the long arms of Los Angeles' Connie Hawkins.

lay-up. He learned the timing that is the key to blocking shots, and he learned to make maximum use of his huge body to push an opponent away from the basket. In short, he graduated from the Russell School of Defense with an "A."

"I didn't teach Bob Lanier anything," said Professor Russell. "I just tried to show him what it takes to win."

Lanier's improved defense fit in perfectly with the philosophy of Detroit coach Ray Scott, who took over the club in the middle of the 1972–73 season. One day before the '73–74 season got underway, Scott telephoned Lanier and invited the big man to his room. "I just want to say that for us to go anywhere at all, we're going to have to play strong defense and that defense is going to have to be initiated by you," Scott told Lanier. "You have a good head on your shoulders, and you're going to have to lead us."

"That's cool," replied Lanier, who went out and followed Scott's game plan with more success than even the coach had dared dream. In Lanier's ill-fated rookie season, the Pistons had allowed 110.9 points per game and finished last in their division. But in 1973–74, led by Lanier's tenacious defense, they allowed only 100.3 points per game, fourth best among the 17 NBA teams. As a result, they finished with that super 52–30 record.

Lanier's all-round ability was a boon to his

teammates. "He took the pressure off the rest of us," said Detroit guard Dave Bing. "He did the things a good basketball team has to have done, and the rest of us were able to concentrate on our own jobs. Bob has earned the respect of every member of this club. We all know it begins and ends with him."

"I don't know if I'm more mature or not," Lanier said after the '73–74 season. "I think I'm a little more disciplined and a little less prone to make the mistakes the average guy at my position would make. I think I'm helping us out in team leadership. And I think I have grown with this team. When I'm going good, the team seems to lift up. Even when I'm not hitting, if I block shots it lifts them, But I can do a lot better. The first year, playing against guys like Kareem Abdul-Jabbar, it was exciting. I was nervous. Now I've adjusted to the schedule and the mental aspects of getting up for a game almost every night. Now they've got to worry about me just as much as I've got to worry about them."

A man can lead in many ways. He can do it with an angry blast or a joke, depending upon the situation, but in either case his action is designed to foster a feeling of unity. Bob got along well with all his teammates, but his special friend was Dave Bing. Lanier and Bing liked to tease each other. The kidding sometimes appeared brutal to outsiders, but the affection and respect the two Piston stars felt for each other never wavered.

"Maybe it wouldn't be that way if we were both guards," explained Lanier. "A competition might develop between us. But the way it is now, David is the guard and I am the center, and it works out well for both of us. I feel sorry for [forward] Curtis Rowe, for instance. The way I play, standing in the middle, I take a lot of his game away from him. He can't drive the way he might if I wasn't there. This has to hurt him in the long run, but with David and myself it is not a problem. Anyway, David and I are complete opposite personalities. I think that's helped keep us together. I need him and he needs me."

Bing was gregarious and outgoing. Lanier tended to be quiet, introspective, and at times moody. But on and off the court, their wildly divergent personalities somehow meshed perfectly. Their friendship dated back to Lanier's senior year at St. Bonaventure. Bing was then a four-year pro. "Right off, we could talk to each other," Bing recalled.

The relationship deepened during Lanier's troubled rookie year. Bing would invite Bob home with him after practice and, following dinner, the two men would sit and discuss basketball and life for hours. Bob was single at the time but was seriously dating Shirley Neville, whom he had met at Bennett High in Buffalo. "He says I was stuck up then," said Shirley, who became Mrs. Lanier on July 24, 1971.

The Bings, Dave and his wife Aaris, took the young couple under their wing and made them feel

Big Bob sets a pick for his friend and teammate Dave Bing (21).

at home in their new community. "No one will ever know what David and his wife meant to us in those early days," said Lanier.

And when Bing needed help in later years, Lanier was ready and eager to do all he could. The star guard of the Pistons suffered a serious eye injury during the 1970–71 season that threatened his career. "When David suffered his eye problems, he lost his confidence," Bob recalled. "He wondered if he'd ever be able to play again. That's when I was able to help him."

In the fall of 1974, Bing became involved in a serious contract dispute with the Pistons. He held out well into the pre-season training period, and his absence threatened the team unity the Pistons had worked so hard to achieve the season before. Lanier recognized the danger and immediately made his giant presence felt.

"If David's not going to be here, it puts that much more responsibility on me to make the big plays," Lanier explained early in '74. "Last year everybody came through at one time or another, but I could always count on Dave to be there. I don't know how long he'll be gone but I'm going to have to do more until he's back. . . . I think I've always been a leader on the floor, but with Dave gone I've talked more with the younger players, making sure they kept their heads in the right direction."

"Bob's been vital," exclaimed a grateful Ray

Scott. "Without Dave here it was necessary for one of the players to step forward and do it . . . keep everybody together, help the kids, things like that. He's really done it. He's emerged as a leader and he's been fantastic."

Bing's holdout finally ended when Lanier invited him over to his house and asked him to return for the good of the team. Bing could say no to management, but he couldn't say no to his close friend and teammate.

Lanier himself had no need to worry about a salary dispute. The year before, in May 1973, his old contract had been torn up and replaced with a new $1.5 million, five-year pact. Under the old contract his income was spread over fifteen years. His new agreement paid him more money more quickly. "It better give me security for a lot more than the next five years," Lanier said.

Lanier invested some of his money in a shopping center in Florida, some apartment buildings, and stocks and bonds. He bought a handsome home in a Detroit suburb, where he lived with his wife, their three children, and the family pet, a big German shepherd.

Lanier's favorite room was his den. It was full of trophies—perhaps 40 in all—tracing the rise of an athletic superstar. Most featured small bronze basketball players, but there was one baseball trophy he had won for pitching the Buffalo Boys Club to a league championship. Two of the trophies stood about four feet tall. One was for winning the 1971–72 NBA One-on-One Championship, and the other is inscribed, "ABA-NBA All-Star Game, May 25, 1972, Most Valuable Player, Bob Lanier."

The newest trophy was the one he received for being voted Most Valuable Player of the 1974 NBA All-Star Game. He earned that handsome piece of hardware by making 11 of 15 shots, including all six of his fourth-quarter attempts. He scored 24 points in the West's 134–123 victory. He also grabbed ten rebounds. The press gave him 29 votes for MVP to 16 for runner-up Spencer Haywood of the Seattle SuperSonics.

When Bob wasn't playing ball, he and his wife often relaxed by going out to movies and to dinner or playing cards with friends. They traveled to Puerto Rico and the Bahamas on vacations and to Monaco with the NBA tour. Everywhere they went, Shirley Lanier said, someone recognized her husband, which was just fine with Bob. "If Bob went out for a day and nobody asked for his autograph or asked if he was Bob Lanier, he'd probably be shattered," she explained with a laugh.

"Bob's a great kidder," she said. "He's always sneaking up on me and tapping me on the shoulder. We have sliding doors in our bedroom, and once when I was in bed and thought the house was empty one of the doors slowly slid open. I was pretty scared until I found out it was Bob."

On the basketball court however, Lanier was all business. Certainly, there were no laughs when he went up against the towering superstar of Milwaukee, the man against whom all NBA centers are measured. Lanier admitted that Abdul-Jabbar had a significant edge in their early meetings, but eventually he learned to hold his own against the big Buck.

"I take him outside and try to drive the hoop more than I do against others," Lanier explained, "because I think you have to go *at* him. Shirley and I discuss him a lot at home, and that's the thing I wasn't able to do when I first came into the league. And then the year after that he had a mental thing over me which is . . . well, it's something to have over another player. He *knew* he could beat me. But he doesn't have that anymore. It's a heads-up thing now. Because if both of us get the ball enough times, both of us are going to score, both of us are going to rebound the same, both of us are going to block shots. Then it's just the rest of the guys helping out, playing defense, that is going to make the difference in who wins and who loses."

Bob McAdoo of Buffalo, Boston's Dave Cowens, and Sam Lacey of the Kansas City–Omaha Kings were the other NBA centers Lanier respected most. "McAdoo has got quickness and such range," he

After going up for a rebound during a 1974 game, Lanier comes down hard on Kings' center Sam Lacey.

said. "He's really a forward playing center, and he handles the ball as well as almost any guard in the league. But what he gets offensively, he's going to give back defensively.

"Cowens is much quicker than I am, and he runs like there's no tomorrow. Therefore, our guards will have to compensate. Like if Cowens gets back too fast on offense, Dave Bing will have to pick him up until I get there. So then I'll slow Dave's man down and then—bang—we'll switch. They're not going to hurt us as long as everybody's protecting everybody else.

"Sam Lacey's a helluva good center," Lanier went on. "He's probably one of the most underrated players in the league."

Surprisingly, it was not always the biggest stars who gave Lanier the most trouble. "Probably somebody like Dennis Awtrey [of Phoenix] or Neal Walk [of the New York Knicks] are toughest for me because they push a lot and get away with it," explained Lanier. "I wish they would do a survey of the things that happen to me on the court. It would be unreal. They would need four refs to watch all the stuff that happens to me."

Steve Patterson of the Cleveland Cavaliers was one of those centers who sometimes gave Lanier a rough time, pushing and shoving the Detroit big man. Lanier usually confined his response to arguing with the officials, but one night he decided to take matters into his own huge hands.

"We were playing in Detroit," the 6-foot-9, 225-pound Patterson recalled. "I'm aware of Lanier's great strength, but I figured I was really playing the guy heads-up, when, suddenly, I don't know how he did it . . . I was leaning on him, hammering him, practically hanging on him, and he just wrapped his arms around me and threw me to the ground like I was a rag doll. It was like I wasn't even there. I did a complete four-point landing, landed on both elbows, bruised them both, and they really swelled up.

"Bob didn't even appear to be angry, because as soon as he did it, he looked at me, offered his hand and helped me up. But he gave me a graphic illustration that, all right, you can play rough and you can play strong, but there is a line past which you cannot go."

Lanier's moments of violence were rare, however. Most of the time he looked a lot fiercer than he really was. Still, he could be a pretty intimidating sight, especially when he went into one of his mock rages.

"Why is it none of you believe me when I tell you I'm the best center around?" he roared in the locker room before one 1975 game, pounding the padded trainer's table for emphasis. Strangers to Lanier were scurrying for the exit, but they stopped as soon as they saw his angry scowl dissolve into a broad grin.

"I'm just trying to do my job," he said. "You've

got to do something during the course of a season or you'd go bananas out there. So you play little mind games, trying to psych yourself into playing better. You tell yourself you're the best offensive player. Then you tell yourself you're the best defensive player. Then you tell yourself you give out the most assists. . . ." Lanier paused, then broke out laughing. "And you know that's not me!"

Someone asked the big man about his ultimate aim in basketball. Lanier's grin instantly changed to a serious, thoughtful expression. "I want to be known as the best in my profession," he said. "I want to be respected as a player and as a man. The fans, I suppose, will never get to know me as a man, so all I can offer them is myself as a player."

And as thousands of Detroit fans came to realize, Bob Lanier had quite a lot to offer.

"I don't feel like I've been in a basketball game unless I have bloody knees."

Dave Cowens

The ball, last touched by the Boston Celtics, was going out of bounds. The huge crowd that was jammed into Madison Square Garden to watch the Knickerbockers battle the visiting Celtics in a December 1974 game was sure the Knicks were about to gain possession. So was the man closest to the ball, Knick guard Earl Monroe. He stood near the end line watching it sail out of bounds, his hands raised in the player's classic "I didn't touch it" position.

Suddenly, a body sailed past Monroe. Boston center Dave Cowens wasn't about to concede the Knicks possession. His face as red as his flaming hair, Cowens made a guided missile of his muscular 230-pound body. He hurled himself after the ball with no thought of the possibly painful consequences.

For a breathtaking moment, Cowens seemed to hang suspended in space. Then he grabbed the ball and flung it high in the air onto the court behind him. His body, of course, kept moving forward—and didn't stop until it landed on top of a fan in the fifth row of the arena.

The other nine players on the court were so caught up in Cowens' flight that they almost forgot the ball was back in play (it was caught by Celtic guard Jo Jo White). The thousands of spectators Cowens didn't land on—diehard Knick fans, who normally would rather cut off their hands than applaud a Celtic—burst into spontaneous applause at the big redhead's display of determination. Only Cowens seemed unimpressed with his feat. To him it was all in a night's work.

"I don't feel like I've been in a basketball game unless I have bloody knees," he explained later. In pro basketball, a floorburn is a badge of honor that indicates a player's willingness to sacrifice some skin to gain a loose ball. And throughout his NBA career, Cowens led the league in floorburns. "I really don't think you can play this game well unless you're aggressive," said Cowens.

Dave Cowens was more than aggressive. He played basketball with a fury that bordered on the maniacal. "You can hardly even talk to Dave during a game," said fiery Boston coach Tom Heinsohn. "I'm way up to here during a game, but he's about

Boston's Dave Cowens is only 6-foot-8, but he's head and shoulders above the crowd when it comes to rebounding.

two times higher. Sometimes I speak right at him during a time-out and I know he's trying to listen, but he just doesn't hear."

Cowens didn't dispute Heinsohn's words. "Every time we get off the bench to resume the game, I've learned to ask [teammate] John Havlicek what play we're going to run," he admitted with a grin.

Pro basketball players play 82 regular-season games. None of them expect to win them all, with one exception—Dave Cowens. "You can't play one good game and one bad one," he said. "It makes no difference that we've won more than eighty percent of our games, either. I don't understand that kind of thinking. I don't want to lose any games. If I say to myself, 'We'll probably win 60 of the 82 games,' we'll win 40. You have to set that goal as high as possible. I know that sooner or later we're going to lose, but I don't expect to lose any games. Do you think it makes sense to go out and say, 'Well, maybe we'll lose tonight, but that's okay, we have to lose sooner or later'? It doesn't make any sense to me."

Cowens' hustle and seemingly boundless energy were matched only by his incredible speed. He was relatively small to be an NBA center (6-foot-8), but his speed and desire helped him become one of the league's brightest young stars. "I feel less talented than a lot of the players I play against," Dave admitted. "And I know that most of them are a lot taller. But I can run the hundred-yard dash with anyone in the league. To be effective, I've got to use my speed all the time. I've got to force the bigger guys out of their usual patterns and into mine by making them afraid that I'll run away from them and score easy baskets. They weren't always so conscious of my speed, but they seem very conscious of it now. They're chasing me harder all the time. I started running because I didn't want them to embarrass me, and now they're running so I won't embarrass them."

Cowens' speed gave him a defensive mobility bigger centers lacked. "Dave's unbelievably quick for a center," said teammate Jo Jo White. "He comes way out from under the basket, and he'll switch and put his hand in the other guy's face. Lots of centers don't like to come way out. They'll move out a little bit and then sag right back. So all a shooter has to do is hesitate, wait for the center to drop back, and then move behind the screen and shoot. With Dave around, guards really don't want any part of that monster shouting at them and waving his arm. They want to pick up the ball and get rid of it. And that gives us a chance to knock the ball away and run a fast break.

His opponents often felt as if they'd played a doubleheader after facing Cowens in basketball's version of the Boston Marathon. "I'll tell you, it's not a whole lot of fun playing against him," admitted Otto Moore of the New Orleans Jazz. "After Boston has played three games in a row you would think Dave would be tired, but he just doesn't tire. Up and down, up and down, up and down. He never stops."

"Cowens is the toughest man I've ever played against," said Nate Thurmond, veteran center of the Chicago Bulls. "By that I don't mean he's the best, just the toughest. He's a new breed of center who's proven that six-foot-eight is big enough in a given situation."

"He adds a different threat to Boston's game," added Chicago guard Norm Van Lier. "He has great defensive range on the horizontal rather than the vertical. He'll meet me at the top of the key, spread those long arms, and make it almost impossible to pass off without his getting a finger on the ball."

No one knew Cowens' strengths better than the man who scouted, drafted, then signed him for the Celtics. "Dave Cowens has brought a new dimension to the game," said Boston general manager Red Auerbach. "He's a center who plays forward. He's a forward who plays center. He's a big man and a little man. He has size and speed. He's going to make other clubs start looking for guys like him."

Auerbach was one of Dave's most enthusiastic fans—with good reason. A look at Boston's record just before Cowens joined them and their record since then will explain that enthusiasm. After winning 11 championships in 13 seasons, the greatest dynasty in professional sports history had crumbled in 1969 with the retirement of super-center Bill Russell, the great Celtic leader who elevated defense to an art form in pro basketball. With the willing but not always very able Henry Finkel at center, the Celtics finished the 1969–70 season with a dismal 34–48 record and failed to make the post-season playoffs for the first time in 19 years.

The following year, however, Cowens came to Boston and turned the Celtics around. They immediately improved ten full games, finishing the 1970–71 season with a 44–38 record. In the next four years, Boston won four consecutive Atlantic Division championships and one NBA title (1973–74). It seemed that a new Celtic dynasty was in the making. This time, however, the center and heart of the team was Dave Cowens.

In his first five seasons as a pro, Cowens averaged 17, 18.8, 20.5, 19.0, and 20.4 points per game, and 15.1, 15.2, 14.9, 15.7 and 14.7 rebounds. A durable performer, he missed only six of 328 regular-season games in his first four years. Then he was forced to sit out the first 17 games of the 1974–75 season with a broken foot. Without Cowens, the defending champion Celtics limped along at a .500 pace but spurted to their accustomed perch atop the Atlantic Division when he returned.

Shortly after his comeback, Cowens faced the

New York Knicks. If the New Yorkers expected Cowens to show any signs of weakness, they were in for a rude shock. "I regret to say that Cowens looked like his old self," said Knick coach Red Holzman after watching Cowens score 23 points and pull down 14 rebounds.

Although Cowens' scoring and rebounding were obvious assets, it was on defense that he really shone. There again, his chief weapons were quickness, aggressiveness, determination, and energy.

"If I score, fine, but a center's job is to captain the defense," Cowens said. "He calls the switches and screens, and he's the last line of defense. If the man he's guarding gets by him, he's got a lay-up. So I concentrate on defense, and let the points fall where they may. It's hard work, but it's fun, too. Rebounding and blocking out are the guts of the game. The fans don't always know what you're doing, but your fellow players on both teams do. Maybe that's why I enjoy defense so much.

"The play is fast and you have to communicate with your teammates, helping each other out on switches, screens, rebounds, and all the other strategies that make up pro ball. It's not just a simple matter of guarding your man. You're responsible for the whole team.

"I prefer defense to offense," Cowens went on. "Not that I'm comparing myself to Bill Russell, who was the best defensive center in basketball. I'll

Cowens outhustles Buffalo's Gar Heard for a rebound.

probably never be as good defensively as Russell because I just don't have the physical capabilities. But I'm a better offensive player than he was. I can shoot better.

"People who think I'm too small to play center are very wrong. They say I'm a natural forward because of my height—that at six-foot-eight I give away too many inches to be effective against the seven-footers. Well, I'm not going to move to forward unless somebody is good enough to beat me out of my job at center."

Cowens had already proven that it takes more than height to be an effective center, and no one was about to challenge him for the job. But people who knew him back when he was a freshman at Catholic High School in Newport, Kentucky, would have laughed at the idea of his becoming a big man and playing the pivot. That's because he was not particularly tall for his age and, until his junior year, showed no great interest in basketball.

The second of six children born to a Newport barber and his wife, Dave preferred baseball and swimming to basketball. "Only" six feet tall as a sophomore, he didn't even try out for the Newport basketball team. Instead, he competed in the 100-yard backstroke and 200-yard freestyle for the swimming team.

After shooting up five inches the summer before his junior year, Dave finally decided to give basketball a try. At first, he was placed on the reserves, or junior varsity, where he gave an early display of the famed Cowens stamina.

"Our second game, I played the full four quarters for the reserves," he recalled. "The varsity game came right after, and I played another three quarters of it. From then on, I was a starter with the varsity."

Right from the beginning, Cowens put all of his considerable energy into the game. "I credit my coach, Jim Connor, with helping me develop my scrambling style of play," he said years later. "He made me cover guards, so I had to learn to stay with my man, reach in, and try to steal the ball and still not foul. Too many coaches simply don't teach a tall guy the whole game. They just try to take advantage of his height.

"We played a fast-break, pressing-defense game. I'd go from harassing an inbounds pass to picking up the ballhandler to running back to halfcourt. It's the way I learned to play basketball, the only way I've ever played, and the only way I like to play."

Averaging 13 points and 20 rebounds per game, Cowens led Newport to a 29–3 record and a spot in the state championship playoffs in his senior year. Scholarship offers came in from a number of colleges, including Louisville and Cincinnati. But Cowens chose little-known Florida State, mainly because coach Hugh Durham emphasized that his school *did not* have a strong basketball program.

"I wasn't sure I could make it in college ball," Dave explained, "but coach Durham promised I'd start as a sophomore. I did get my chance to start right away, and I never regretted my decision to go to Florida State one bit. Everything's been roses since then."

With Dave in the pivot, Florida State posted a 59–19 record in three seasons and developed into a major college basketball power. Cowens averaged 18.9 points and 17 rebounds per game, making an impressive 51.9 percent of his shots. In his senior year, team captain Cowens led F.S.U. to an outstanding 23–3 record. The highlight of his college career came against Jacksonville, F.S.U.'s arch rival. The Jacksonville players had not lost a game all season. And with 7-foot-2 Artis Gilmore at center, they didn't plan to lose this one either. But they didn't reckon with Dave Cowens. He spent the week before the game shooting over tennis rackets held up by teammates to simulate the long, long arms of Gilmore. Well-prepared for the contest, Cowens wound up popping in 19 points over Gilmore and did a masterful defensive job on the big man—and Florida State wound up with a big win.

"There may be better shooters, better rebounders, better defensive players, but I doubt there is anyone who can do so many things as well as Dave," said the grateful coach Durham just before his star graduated.

Celtic general manager Red Auerbach scouted Cowens and came back raving. "Red made a big display of walking out after five minutes, hoping people would think he was disappointed," recalled Celtic coach Tom Heinsohn. " 'Tommy,' he told me when he got back, 'I found the kid we want.' "

"You know, Cowens scared me the first time I scouted him," Auerbach said. "He was so good that I kept hoping he'd make a mistake. There were scouts from a half-dozen other NBA teams in that building, and I figured if they saw the same potential in Cowens that I did, I was dead."

Auerbach held his breath when the 1970 draft began. Detroit took Bob Lanier. Atlanta picked Pete Maravich. The San Diego Rockets (who later moved to Houston) took Rudy Tomjanovich. Only then did Auerbach relax. It was Boston's turn. It took him a half-second to shout, "Boston takes Dave Cowens of Florida State!"

Cowens threw himself into preparing for his professional career with characteristic energy and determination. He joined summer leagues in Boston and New York, playing as many as six games per week. He played in Harlem's famous Rucker Tournament, competing against many top pros. Finally, Auerbach and Heinsohn told him to relax a little. They were afraid their ferocious rookie would exhaust himself before training camp even started. "We were afraid he would go stale," Heinsohn said.

Cowens looked anything but stale at the Maurice Stokes benefit game that summer. The benefit was an annual pro all-star game played at Kutsher's Country Club in Monticello, New York. For many years the proceeds went to Maurice Stokes, a pro star who had been stricken with crippling encephalitis in 1958 at the height of his tragically brief NBA career. (After Stokes' death in 1973, the event continued for the benefit of other injured former players.)

Everyone at the 1970 Stokes game was anxious to get a look at "Pistol" Pete Maravich, the flamboyant, colorful, high-scoring rookie of the Atlanta Hawks. Before the game, Maravich put on a flashy show of tricks with the basketball. But then the game began, and Cowens put on an even better show. Going in at forward late in the opening quarter, he gave NBA opponents a preview of things to come with his constant movement, defensive muscle, surprisingly delicate shooting touch, and hustle. By the time the game was over, Cowens had scored 32 points (a record for the Stokes game) and grabbed 22 rebounds. He was voted the game's Most Valuable Player.

Everyone was awed by Cowens' performance—except the big redhead himself. "Most of the other guys weren't in shape yet," he modestly observed. "The reason that I did better than usual was that I was in shape. It's bound to make a difference. I was

Dave relaxes in the Celtics' locker room after a Boston victory.

getting up and down the court faster, I scored most of my points on offensive tip-ins. I'm not going to get cocky or big-headed about an exhibition game. It didn't count toward anything."

The game counted for quite a lot as far as general manager Auerbach was concerned. It showed that Cowens cared enough about looking good to take even a "meaningless" exhibition seriously. It was a good sign that he had what Auerbach called "the Celtic attitude," a combination of pride, competitiveness, aggressiveness, and dedication.

"Dave was always a very dedicated kid," said Auerbach. "Now a dedicated kid isn't unheard of, but there aren't as many around as we would like. Our problem with Cowens is telling him to lay off. He does too much."

As the Celtics began their pre-season training camp, only one real question remained about Cowens: what position should he play? At 6-foot-8, he'd be smaller than almost all the other centers in the NBA (and at least six inches smaller than the league's dominant giant, Kareem Abdul-Jabbar of Milwaukee).

"When I first scouted Dave at Florida State, I didn't have any doubts about his future as a pro," said Auerbach. "But my original estimate was that he'd probably have to be a forward and part-time center.

"What changed my mind was his strength and the

way he jumped in training camp. Then there was his attitude. You could see that nobody was going to tell this kid he couldn't do something if he wanted to do it, and Cowens obviously wanted to play center.

"However, just to make sure, Tommy Heinsohn and I decided to bring in Bill Russell for an opinion. 'Forget his height and play him right where he is,' Russell said. 'You won't be sorry because nobody is going to intimidate this kid. He may need a little time to get ready, but he'll do the job for you.'"

Cowens was more than ready to show what he could do. The pre-season period, with its two-a-day practices and exhibitions, seemed endless to the Celtic rookie. "I was anxious for the regular season to get started," he recalled. "I found the more I waited, the more nervous I got. I spent part of the summer that year sleeping on a mat in the den in [teammate] Don Nelson's apartment. In training camp I had a large color television put in my room to get rid of some of the boredom. I wanted my pro career to start already."

The regular season finally began. But although the Celtics realized he was champing at the bit, they were in no hurry to use Cowens as a starter. "We didn't want Dave to think he had to do everything right away," Heinsohn explained. "We knew he would be able to do a big job for us, but we wanted to keep everything in perspective. So we used him coming off the bench at the start."

In 1970, the redheaded rookie shoots over Laker Happy Hairston.

Cowens' career as a Celtic sub lasted exactly three games—and Boston lost all three. Then, in game four, Cowens replaced Henry Finkel as the starting center. The Celtics picked up their first victory of the season, a 133–115 win over Portland. From that day on, Cowens was a starter.

Of course, it wasn't quite that simple. Cowens was still a rookie who made rookie mistakes. In two areas, ballhandling and outside shooting, he showed clear deficiencies. Still, the Celtics were not worried.

"He'll get better in his ballhandling," Heinsohn told reporters, "and you know his shooting is going to be real good sooner or later. It always was good before, though he'll have to take more outside shots here than he was used to taking in college. But you just look at his style and you know he's going to do it. He just looks like a good shooter."

Cowens himself was very realistic about his abilities. "I don't let my fantasies run away with me," he said. "The pros make very few mistakes. In college you can go through the motions a lot of the time, knowing you're going to beat your man. Here, if you make a mistake, you're going to pay for it.

"I remember one game when Gus Johnson just took me to the cleaners," Dave said, recalling a particularly trying evening against the powerful, agile forward of the then Baltimore Bullets. "I'd come out, he'd drive right by me. I'd hang back, he'd shoot over me. But it's just things like that you learn about the game that help you get better."

Cowens also had some things to learn about offense. "I had an attitude, a feeling I never was a shooter, that I couldn't shoot a lick," he recalled. "I don't know why. I'd have a shot and I wouldn't take it. My teammates told me, 'You've got to shoot. It'll come. You might miss ten in a row, but you'll make it up.' That was something else I had to learn."

Despite his early problems, Cowens had a lot to contribute to the team. Thanks to his 17 points per game, his 15 rebounds (seventh best in the league), and, above all, his fierce defense, the Celtics rebounded from their horrible slide of the 1969–70 season. They won their last four games of '70–71 and missed making the playoffs by just three games.

"We thought we should have made the playoffs," Cowens said, "but we knew we had turned things around in Boston. The people up there who thought that the end of the Russell era meant the end of good teams had to change their minds."

Cowens finished the season in a tie for Rookie of the Year honors with Portland's high-scoring guard, Geoff Petrie. "Cowens deserved to win the whole thing," argued Auerbach. "There shouldn't have been any tie. There was no question that Dave was the best rookie in the league. He would have been the best even if he had only scored ten points a game. We would have been happy with that much scoring because of the tremendous rebounding job he did."

Cowens and the Celtics did an even better job in 1971–72. Boston racked up an impressive 56–26 record, the best in the Atlantic Division, and made it to the semi-finals of the NBA playoffs. Although the young Celtics were finally eliminated by a veteran Knick squad, it was clear that Boston was once again an NBA power to be reckoned with.

In the summer of 1972, the Celtics acquired Paul Silas, one of the game's top rebounding forwards, from Phoenix. Silas proved to be a tremendous asset to the Celtics, particularly to Cowens.

"Paul gave me the chance to free-lance more," Dave explained. "He made it easier for me to play the kind of game I like to play."

"Silas took some of the rebounding and defensive pressure off Dave," added coach Heinsohn. "His presence also let Cowens move out further on offense, and with his outside shooting getting better, it gave our whole offense more variety."

The 1972–73 Celtics had Silas and Cowens banging the boards and providing defensive muscle against opposing big men; veteran forward John Havlicek shooting, running, and defending in all-pro fashion; Jo Jo White shooting his 20 points per game at one guard spot; tenacious defender Don Chaney sticking to the other team's best shooter at the other backcourt position; and Don Nelson, the best sixth man in the league, coming in off the bench. The Celtics ran up an awesome 68–14 record during the regular season, which put them eight games ahead of their closest NBA rivals.

Once more, the Celtics made it to the semi-finals against the Knicks. A shoulder injury to Havlicek, whose 23.8 point-per-game average led the Celtics, kept the all-pro forward on the bench for most of that series. Cowens averaged 24.4 points and 14.1 rebounds in a valiant effort to make up for the crippling loss of Havlicek, the Celtic captain and leader. But the Celtics were finally eliminated in the seventh and final contest. As a reward for his outstanding season, Cowens was voted the league's Most Valuable Player, receiving 67 first-place votes to 33 for runner-up Abdul-Jabbar. Cowens was the first Celtic to receive the honor since Bill Russell won it for the fifth and final time in 1965.

In typical Celtic fashion, Dave went out of his way to praise his teammates when he learned about the award. "We're a great team," he said. "It's easy to win an award when you're surrounded by the type of individuals we have. It means a lot to me to win it, but it means an awful lot more to have your team do well. Otherwise individual awards lose their whole meaning."

In Boston, however, doing well meant nothing less than winning the NBA championship. "They're used to championships here," explained Heinsohn. "This isn't the end for us. We'll be back."

The next year, the Celtics *were* back—all the way

Cowens leaps high in the air in an attempt to keep the Knicks' inbounds pass away from Walt Frazier (10).

back. This time they broke their semi-final jinx and advanced to the finals. There they faced Abdul-Jabbar and his Bucks. After six games the teams were tied with three victories each. Milwaukee had the home-court advantage for the seventh and deciding game, but that didn't seem to bother Cowens or the Celtics. The big redhead outscored his towering rival, 28 to 26, and out-rebounded him, 14 to 13—and Boston won, 102–87.

Soaked with champagne in the winners' locker room after the game, Cowens spoke about the meaning of Boston's victory. "I guess respect is what it's all about," he said, "whether you're talking basketball or life. You've got to do your best for yourself and for those you're working with. My father is a good model because nobody could ever say a bad thing about him. You have respect for yourself and everybody else. It all comes down to the same thing, in sports, your job, school, anything. Do the right thing, don't try to hurt anybody, and it'll all work out fine. I'd say that's a pretty good way to live."

Cowens had some very definite ideas about the way he wanted to live. Like many athletes, he lived two very different kinds of lives. On a basketball court, his drive, energy, and intensity couldn't help but attract attention. Off the court, however, he was strictly low key. He didn't do anything to attract attention because he didn't want any.

Cowens gets a hero's welcome in 1974 as he and the Celtics bring the NBA championship back to Boston.

"One thing's sure, I doubt that I'd want to stay in the public eye once I'm through playing ball," he said. "I'm not saying that playing basketball for a living isn't great. But because you're in the public eye, people are always gushing over you, telling you how great you are and all that mushy malarkey. But I'm no saint.

"People want my autograph. For what? Maybe I'm a jerk. Maybe I'm a heel. How do they know? I'm the type of guy who sometimes loses his temper in a fight. Once when I was in high school I told my parents I was sleeping over at a friend's house and then I drove around all night in a car, drinking beer. But I'm also a guy who tries to do people favors and who is trying to mature, trying to learn as I grow older."

Although Cowens made a great deal of money, his tastes remained simple. He liked to stay at home by himself, reading or listening to records or just relaxing by a fire. He enjoyed cooking, although he was hardly an expert. "I usually make soup or a large ham or a casserole," he said, "something that lasts long." A favorite was a tuna casserole he got off the back of a noodle box. "But it's so good that I once ate three large portions at one meal," he recalled. "Then I got sick." Another time, he called his mother in Kentucky for a new breakfast recipe. "Mom," he said, "how do you make soft-boiled eggs?"

Cowens' taste in automobiles was strictly utilitarian. He preferred the rugged jeep type cars, which suited his love of the outdoors. His clothing was casual—to say the least. "I'm not really big on clothes," he said. "I just sort of grab the first thing I see on the rack and don't pay any attention to what else I'm wearing." And the only reason he ever wore a tie was because Auerbach required his players to wear one.

Money or possessions didn't seem to matter very much to Cowens. "Sure, the money is nice," he admitted, "but it doesn't change the way I live or the things I like. I don't see how it could. I'm still me and I like to live the way I always have liked to live. I don't like to call attention to myself off the court. I can't relate to people that way. On the court, I have to relate to what I'm doing against my opponent. Off the court, I want to be just another person and be treated by what I have to say or do, not by what I may look like or the status people think I have."

The small clapboard bungalow Cowens rented in Weston, Massachusetts, approximately 20 miles outside Boston, suited him perfectly. It contained a rocking chair, a folding chair, and a yellow convertible couch. Seated in his folding chair, Cowens once gave a visitor the grand tour. "That's my living room," he said, pointing to one corner. Then he pointed to the other corners: "Over there is my dining room, and there is my den, and over there is my office, and you're sitting in my bedroom. I've also got a kitchen, a bathroom, and a pretty big closet."

Cowens had found the house through an ad on a bulletin board at Harvard University, where he was taking a course in his spare time. It had been placed by Richard and Phyliss Gold, upon whose estate the bungalow was located. The Golds thought it might be suitable for a professor or student at a nearby college. Instead, they got one of the finest basketball players in the world for a tenant. When Cowens saw the ad, he immediately called the Golds.

"Have you got a house to rent?" he asked.

"Yes," answered Phyliss Gold.

"Rented yet?"

"No, but . . ."

"Can I look?"

"Yes, but who are you—a student?"

"No."

"What are you, then?"

"I play basketball."

"Oh, that's nice. We have a net right out here in the driveway. Do you think you could tell me who you play basketball for?"

"For Boston."

"You mean you're a *Celtic*?"

"I had been a great fan of the Celtics when Bob Cousy was with the team," Phyliss Gold later explained. "But we hadn't paid much attention to the team since Cousy left. Neither Richard nor I knew who Dave Cowens was. Anyway, I told him to come over. A little later this big, gorgeous redhead was standing at my door. I called Richard and told him we had rented the house to a Celtic. Richard asked me, 'Does he have a no-cut contract?' "

The Golds later became Cowens' closest friends in Boston. Dave was like an older brother to their three teenage children, and Richard Gold, a lawyer-businessman, became Dave's financial adviser. Among Dave's investments were apartment houses in Baltimore, a catfish farm in British Honduras, and a farm in Newport, Kentucky, where he thought he might someday retire.

Dave also considered such varied post-basketball careers as owning a service station and acting as its mechanic, going into criminology (his major in college), or coaching. "I think a lot about my life after basketball," he said. "I'm not going to play all my life. And I doubt whether I could remain involved in the game on a serious level. If I ever coached, it would probably be on the high school level. I wouldn't want to go higher. I wouldn't want to get involved in the pressure and politics of it, the recruiting. I'd want boys to come out for my team, and I'd take what I got and try to mold them into a team."

Whatever Cowens decided to do, it seemed almost certain that he would do it out in the country. His love of wide open spaces was what led him to live in Weston instead of Boston.

"For one thing, you can be free out here," he

The league-leader in floor burns, Dave picks up a few more during a hard-fought game.

explained. "I mean if I want to run outside and holler and scream and go crazy, I can. I haven't yet, but the option is always open.

"Secondly, I don't like the city and living in an apartment house. There you're like an automaton. You press the elevator button to take you up to your apartment, which looks like everyone else's apartment. You have your designated parking space. And the traffic! As soon as the light turns green the car behind you honks . . .

"Sometimes friends visit me out here. Sometimes I take walks through the woods, or I walk about a mile and a half into town, or I go fishing at my pond, which is filled with bass and pickerel—every time you cast you catch something. I don't tell anybody else where the pond is. I keep it my private fishing hole.

"Being out in the country like I am gives you a perspective. You think about being idolized because you're a basketball player. That's absurd. A basketball player is nothing important. He really doesn't contribute to making people's lives happier—not like a plumber or a fireman or even a businessman."

Fans of basketball in general, and the Celtics in particular, would hardly agree with that last statement. The artistry and intensity with which the Celtics and their big man played the game had certainly made millions of people happy.

Bob McAdoo

The young athletes of Greensboro, North Carolina, like young athletes everywhere, want to be like the pros. It might be 30 degrees and snowing, but when the major leaguers report to spring training, gloves, bats, and balls emerge in Greensboro. Likewise, it could be 90 degrees in the Greensboro shade when the pro football season begins, but away go the baseballs and out come the footballs. A few months later, the footballs suddenly disappear and are replaced by basketballs. And so it goes.

Bob McAdoo faithfully followed the seasons in Greensboro until the fall of his sophomore year at Ben L. Smith High School. But that year, when the baseball season was officially put to rest, McAdoo did not follow the crowd to football. Instead, he proceeded directly to basketball—with good reason. He had just shot up four inches to stand a towering 6-foot-8, but he hadn't filled out at all. He looked like a giant pencil, and his family was afraid he might get snapped in two if he continued to play football.

"I was always getting hurt playing football, so some uncles of mine told me I should lay off the game because I was too frail," McAdoo recalled. "But with my new height, I found I could easily shoot over everyone so I began concentrating on basketball."

Years later, McAdoo was still shooting over everyone. The then 6-foot-9, 210-pound star center of the Buffalo Braves was considered perhaps the finest shooting big man in basketball history. In 1972–73, he was named NBA Rookie of the Year. The next season, the 22-year-old McAdoo became the youngest scoring champion in league history, with an average of 30.6 points per game. And the following year, he defended that title with a 34.5-point average and was honored as the NBA's Most Valuable Player. He sank a league-leading 54.7 percent of his shots as a soph and 51.2 percent in his third season. It was the quality as much as the quantity of shots that made McAdoo so great. For his were not the normal five-foot hooks, tap-ins, and lay-ups most centers rely on for their points. For the most part, McAdoo was a long-range bomber, deadly from distances up to 25 feet.

McAdoo's accuracy was really amazing when you consider exactly what's involved in sinking a typical 20-foot jump shot. What the shooter must do is toss a ball almost 10 inches in diameter 20 feet through a metal ring only 18 inches in diameter extended 10 feet in the air. That doesn't leave much room for error—especially in a tense, pressure-filled game situation.

Although his shooting tended to overshadow everything else, McAdoo also contributed to the Braves in all the other ways a center should. He ranked third and fourth in rebounding in his second and third seasons, grabbing an average of 15.1 and 14.1 per game. Some observers felt his defense was hampered by his lack of bulk, especially when he had to contend with giants like Milwaukee's Kareem Abdul-Jabbar (7-foot-2, 245 pounds) and Detroit's Bob Lanier (6-foot-11, 260 pounds). But if the bigger centers' muscle presented McAdoo with problems, his quickness, moves, and incredible scoring range gave them plenty of headaches in return.

And woe to the guard or forward bold enough to attempt a drive through the middle of the Braves' defense. Buffalo Bob was quick to switch to someone else's man on defense and slam the shot back into his face. But with the occasional exception of Abdul-Jabbar, who, when fully extended, could block anyone's shots, no one blocked McAdoo.

"He's like an ancient Greek god," Los Angeles Laker forward Bill Bridges once said, after chasing

McAdoo for a harrowing 33 minutes one night. "He's Mercury out there. He makes all those mythical things I've always heard about happen. The game is easy for him. He scores thirty against Jabbar, thirty against Thurmond, thirty against Cowens. And he hasn't even reached his peak yet."

"When you think you've got McAdoo where you want him—watch out," cautioned Seattle Super-Sonic coach Bill Russell, the former great Boston Celtic center who has seen or played against all the game's top big men over the past 20 years. "He takes the seventeen-footer you want him to take—but they go in." Russell had just watched McAdoo sink 21 baskets in 28 attempts and scored 49 points in a 1975 game against the Sonics.

Two years earlier, against Russell's old Boston team, Big Mac made 21 baskets in 29 shots and scored 52 points. He swished them in, banked them in, and stuffed them in, leaving the hard-to-impress Celtics singing his praises.

"It was an incredible feat," said veteran forward Paul Silas. "He hit nothing but net. I think Spencer Haywood is unstoppable sometimes, but McAdoo is unbelievable."

"I don't think I've ever seen a better shot anywhere," said Boston's other veteran forward, Don Nelson. "His quick release is unbelievable."

"He always can get off his shot," said guard Paul Westphal. "I once blocked his shot from behind, but

Buffalo super-shooter Bob McAdoo soars to the basket while the Bullet defenders watch from below.

he yanked the ball away, hung in the air, and still threw it in."

Another Celtic guard, Jo Jo White, made his tribute short and sweet: "I'm going to call him Mr. McAdoo."

One of the keys to McAdoo's great success as a scorer was his confidence in his shot. Like most standout athletes, McAdoo had a world of faith in his ability. Unlike most, however, Big Mac candidly admitted just how good he thought he was. One reporter, who was used to the "Aw shucks, it was nothing" sort of comment from athletes, was startled when he interviewed McAdoo.

Reporter: "Were you surprised when you were named Rookie of the Year?"

McAdoo: "No. I felt I deserved it."

Reporter: "What are the weak parts of your game?"

McAdoo: "I think I do well in all phases of the game."

Reporter: "There's no one aspect of basketball you feel you need to work on more?"

McAdoo: "No, not really."

Reporter: "Do you think you're underrated?"

McAdoo: "Yes, I think I'm underrated. Maybe it's because I play in Buffalo. It'll be different if we win the championship, though. That's what I want most."

Reporter: "Did you ever lack confidence in your ability?"

McAdoo: "No."
Reporter: "Never?"
McAdoo: "Never."

Not even as a skinny 6-foot-8 high school sophomore did Bob McAdoo doubt he was better than the next guy. And why should he? He always was better.

"I had a happy childhood," said McAdoo. "I was always playing ball. My father was a carpenter and my mother taught first grade. I have only one sister and no brothers. I didn't feel we lacked for anything."

Until his uncles urged him to give up football, young Bob excelled in all sports. Afterward, he stuck to basketball and track. A high jumper, McAdoo's best high school leap was an impressive 6 feet, $8\frac{3}{4}$ inches.

In his three varsity seasons at Smith High, Bob averaged 15, 23, and 25 points per game. As a senior, he hauled down an average of 17 rebounds. College recruiters camped on his doorstep, but Bob chose to first attend Vincennes (Indiana) Junior College and then transfer to a four-year school.

"I didn't visit too many places that tried to recruit me," he explained. "Vincennes was the last place I went to. I really liked all the guys on the team there once I got a chance to meet them. And they were all good ballplayers.

"I also didn't want to go through that freshman schedule at a four-year school [at that time, freshmen were not allowed to play varsity ball]. I wanted to start right off playing tough competition. Vincennes played something like thirty or thirty-five games as opposed to about fifteen for a freshman team at a four-year school. I was planning to transfer after my first season at Vincennes, but they had a real good group of guys coming in for my sophomore year, so I decided to stay and play another season. Junior college was a lot of fun to me."

In his first junior college year, Big Mac averaged 20 points per game and led his team to the national junior college championship. The following year, he raised his scoring average to 25.5 points and grabbed 17 rebounds per game. Vincennes was upset in a regional playoff game and failed to defend its national title.

By the time McAdoo was ready to transfer to a four-year college, the recruiters were back again in force. "I had to go through that whole scene again," Bob recalled. "I enjoyed it at first, but after a while those calls at all times of the day and at night when you're trying to sleep . . ."

McAdoo wanted to go back home, so he picked the University of North Carolina. "I wanted my parents to get a chance to see me play," he explained. "I also liked Dean Smith and John Lotz [the North Carolina head and assistant coaches] real well and I had just watched them win the NIT on television. I knew they'd have a good team the next year because everyone was coming back except the center. It was perfect for me."

An interesting footnote for those who felt UCLA had completely cornered the market on talent during those years when the Bruins were in the midst of their record string of national championships: McAdoo was a big one that got away. Letters expressing UCLA's interest in him were sent to McAdoo, but he never received them. In fact, he didn't learn about the letters until after he had committed himself to North Carolina. Might he have gone to UCLA? "If I had known in time, I certainly would have gone out there for a visit," McAdoo said. "If I had liked the place . . . who knows?"

UCLA's loss was North Carolina's gain. McAdoo was entering his junior year when he enrolled at Carolina. With him at center, the Tar Heels won five tournaments, finished with a 26–5 record, and wound up second to UCLA in the national rankings. "McAdoo turned a good team into a great one," recalled George Karl, a guard on that North Carolina team who went on to play for the San Antonio Spurs in the ABA.

North Carolina was anticipating bigger and better things the following year with McAdoo due back for his senior season; but the Tar Heels were in for a big letdown. Bob decided to give up his final year of college eligibility and turn pro.

Playing college ball for North Carolina in 1971, McAdoo gets off a shot.

"The money was too good to turn down," he said. "Besides, I had had a good year and didn't want to take a chance on an injury the following season that might hurt my chances of playing pro ball. I had an injury playing for the United States team at the Pan-Am Games right before I went to North Carolina that scared me to death. I had a cracked ankle, but the people at the Pan-Am Games told me I just had strained ligaments. So I played with a broken ankle. It bothered me halfway through the year at North Carolina. It wasn't until I had it x-rayed at North Carolina that I learned exactly what was wrong. I didn't want something like that to happen again. I saw my chances and I left."

Bob was drafted by the Virginia Squires of the ABA. The Portland Trail Blazers, who had the number one NBA draft pick, were afraid Bob would sign with the ABA team, so they drafted someone else. That gave the Braves the chance to pick McAdoo, which they did. As it turned out, McAdoo never had the slightest intention of signing with the Squires. "I wanted the NBA because it was a chance to play against guys I followed every week on TV," he said. "I wanted to play against the best."

He never had any doubts that he would make the grade as a pro. "I knew I could play," he said. "I played every summer in pick-up games back home against the Carolina Cougars [later known as the Denver Nuggets] and I had no problems. I played against guys like Doug Moe, Bill Buntin, Charlie Scott, Larry Miller—a lot of the guys who had gone to North Carolina in the past."

But McAdoo, who had excelled at every level of basketball he had ever tried, was in for a rude shock. The Braves already had a starting center in 7-foot-1 Elmore Smith, so McAdoo was switched to a forward spot. And because he was the quickest of the Brave forwards, he was assigned to guard the other teams' smaller, faster forwards—sharpshooters like Altanta's Lou Hudson and New York's Bill Bradley. It's tough enough for a rookie to learn to play defense in the NBA under normal circumstances, but McAdoo was starting with two big handicaps. He was playing a new, unfamiliar position, and he was attempting to cover men several inches shorter—and a lot faster—than himself. The big rookie found it impossible to keep up with his opponents and was frequently embarrassed as they raced by him for easy baskets.

"I played center all my life," he complained, "and then they put me at forward and asked me to guard quick guys. You just don't see six-foot-ten players guarding guys like Bill Bradley."

"It was difficult for Bob to learn that you can't score a basket and then lope back downcourt on defense," said Buffalo general manager Eddie Donovan. "In this league, if you lope on defense the opposition's offense already has formed and your man is putting the ball in the hoop."

McAdoo's whole game suffered, and he frequently found himself on the bench. In the first 29 games of the season, he averaged just 9.5 points per game and was making a poor 36 percent of his shots. He was hurt, confused, and angry. "I was crying inside," he recalled. "I couldn't take it. I wasn't too friendly with the other players. I had a problem with people. I wouldn't mingle too much. I was always teed off."

McAdoo's frustration was noted by the Braves' management. "I've been with four pro basketball teams and I've never seen a rookie as intense as McAdoo," said Rudy Martzke, who was then Buffalo's public relations director. "Most players who join a pro club have been big stars in high school and college and have trouble getting used to sitting on a bench. When they are told repeatedly that it will take at least a year for them to work into a spot, they grudgingly accept it. Not McAdoo. He was downright sullen. Like a lot of big shooters, he had to learn how to move without the ball—among other things. But he wouldn't accept the fact that he wasn't ready to be a starter, and it was clear he was never going to accept the fact that he might not get to play more than ten minutes a game.

"Then on December 16, 1972—I'll never forget the day—he played twenty-two minutes and got thirty points and sixteen rebounds. After that, it was all downhill to the Rookie of the Year award. But he still didn't forget those early games."

McAdoo started the last 51 games of the season and averaged 22.8 points and 10.8 rebounds per game, sinking 48 percent of his shots. That raised his stats for the year to 18 points per game and 9.1 rebounds. In 14 of those last 51 games, he scored 30 or more points, and twice he went over the 40-point mark. In the last three games of the season, the rampaging rookie scored 39, 39, and then 45 points (a team record). Why the complete turnabout? "Just additional playing time, that's all," McAdoo said. "I couldn't understand why I wasn't playing more. I still can't understand it."

Winning the Rookie of the Year award cheered McAdoo up—somewhat. "After the disappointing year we had [a 21–61 record], that was about the only thing I had to be happy about," he said. "And I almost didn't get a chance to win it because I wasn't playing."

But better times lay ahead for both McAdoo and the Braves. In a series of moves that demonstrated why he was considered the shrewdest executive in all of pro basketball, general manager Donovan rebuilt the team for the 1973–74 season. He traded huge but slow Elmore Smith to Los Angeles for sleek, swift forward Jim McMillian; drafted and signed flashy, playmaking Providence guard Ernie

As he drives to the basket in a 1974 game, McAdoo is momentarily stopped—and fouled—by Kansas City's Sam Lacey.

DiGregorio, giving the Braves a badly needed floor leader; and obtained forward Garfield Heard from the Chicago Bulls. Then, in a deal that provided Buffalo with invaluable bench strength, he got forward Jack Marin and guard Matt Goukas from Houston.

When the season began, Buffalo's tentative starting center was Bob Kauffman, a 6-foot-8, 240-pound veteran who had also played forward while Smith was with the club. But when Kauffman suffered a groin pull during the exhibition season, McAdoo moved into the pivot. In the season opener, Big Mac sank a long jump shot at the final buzzer to give Buffalo a 107–105 victory over the Houston Rockets. He wound up with 31 points and 21 rebounds that night and was off and gunning. Kauffman's career as the Braves' center was over before it started.

McAdoo played with a frenzy, as if he were trying to make up for all those nights on the bench he had suffered through as a rookie. He scored over 40 points 10 times and more than 30 points 43 times in the 80 regular-season games in which he participated. In his "worst" game that season, he scored 15 points. The Buffalo big man was runner-up to Kareem Abdul-Jabbar in the league's Most Valuable Player voting. "I deserved the award," said McAdoo, stating an opinion shared by his fans and teammates.

Thanks largely to McAdoo, Buffalo had won 21 more games than in 1972–73 to finish the season with a 42–40 record. For the first time in their four-year history, the Braves made the playoffs. They gave the Boston Celtics (the eventual NBA champions) a tremendous battle before losing a best-of-seven opening round in six games. The series was tied at two games apiece before Boston eked out victories by three and two points, respectively.

Rallying behind the slogan "It's a Brave New World," Bob and the Braves got off to a fast start in 1974–75. They took an early lead in the tough Atlantic Division. The New York Knicks were on the receiving end of a McAdoo blitz the weekend of December 13–14, 1974. The New Yorkers, NBA champions in 1969 and playoff finalists in 1973, had been hurt badly by the retirement of All-Stars Willis Reed and Dave DeBusschere. Now they were trying for one last hurrah. They had won their last six games and were just one game behind Buffalo as they prepared for a home-and-home series against the Braves, two games within a 17-hour span.

It was the classic confrontation between the old champion hoping to hang on for one more taste of glory, and the hungry young challenger. In the first of the two games, the Knicks held an 11-point lead with 9 minutes and 13 seconds to play. Then McAdoo struck. With the home Buffalo crowd roaring encouragement, Big Mac scored 14 points in the last quarter toward a game total of 42. The Braves ran off 15 straight points to win, 108–104.

Big Mac and the Braves battle John Gianelli (40) and the New York Knicks during the 1974–75 season.

Mel Davis, the burly young Knick assigned to guard McAdoo for most of the second half, seemed to be in shock after the game. "I tried to put the beef to him because I'm heavier," said Davis. "I was leaning all over him. But he is a superstar. When it got close, he started seeing things his way."

The next afternoon in New York, the Knicks sprinted to an early 20–8 lead, momentarily exciting the rabid fans at Madison Square Garden. But McAdoo soon silenced them. Hitting shots from everywhere, Big Mac scored 23 of his 37 points in the second half and the Braves won easily, 118–102. In the two games, McAdoo racked up 79 points and hauled down 38 rebounds.

"He made a believer out of me," said Mr. Cool of the Knicks, all-pro guard Walt Frazier.

The Knicks limped through the rest of the season, and the Braves improved their record another seven games, finishing with a 49–33 mark and their second playoff berth in a row.

Braves coach Jack Ramsay paid his center basketball's ultimate compliment. "I wouldn't trade Bob McAdoo for the world," Ramsay said without batting an eyelash. "I have infinite respect for Abdul-Jabbar, but I wouldn't trade McAdoo for anybody or any combination of bodies in the world."

The awesome Abdul-Jabbar was the standard by which all centers were measured. Speaking about his Milwaukee rival, McAdoo admitted, "I was intimidated by him my first year and even at the beginning of my second, but I'm not anymore. I think I'm giving the best players, dudes like Bob Lanier and Abdul-Jabbar, as much trouble as they're giving me. I think I go to the hoop as well as anyone. We're running well, and I'm contributing to the fast break.

"I look at it this way. When you're playing against guys like Abdul-Jabbar and Lanier, you're not going to stop them. Nobody stops them, so you just have to do your best. The rest of the centers I just try to stay as close to as possible and also help out my teammates by switching off and picking up other men. They say that because I weigh only two hundred and five to two hundred and ten pounds that I have trouble with Abdul-Jabbar and Lanier—but then, who doesn't?"

With the exception of those two big men, McAdoo's biggest problems came off the court, not on it. One basketball-related activity McAdoo could easily have done without was the frequent air travel necessary during road trips. McAdoo would spend each flight sitting rigidly with his hat pulled over his eyes—and ears—trying to ignore his friend and teammate Randy Smith, who would be whispering such encouraging words as, "Look, the wing's on fire."

McAdoo also felt somewhat uncomfortable with strangers, but that didn't figure to last long. "The more stature he attains as a star, the more he is going

McAdoo goes one-on-one against Milwaukee's Kareem Abdul-Jabbar.

to have to mix with people," said Braves sportscaster Van Miller in 1975. "Right now that's very difficult for him. Last year, I told him that the people running a big sports banquet in Fredonia, New York, wanted him as a head table guest. And there was a fee involved. He agreed, but only on the condition that he would not be asked to speak. There were all sorts of big stars from other sports at the banquet and they all talked. But Bob just took a bow.

"Of course, people who wonder about his attitude in that direction don't take into consideration that he has spent very little time with white people. That might not seem like much of a problem to them because they are Northerners and believe that all discrimination was done away with by law. Well, a law cannot make a sensitive person forget his early experiences."

Invitations to banquets are one sure way of identifying a superstar. So are commercial endorsements. As of early 1975, McAdoo had not done any commercials. It wasn't because he was too shy, either. "I never have been asked," he said. But things changed later that year when Bill Madden, a New York City lawyer, began representing McAdoo. In an article in *Sport* magazine, Madden said, "He had his chance to endorse a line of basketball sneakers. All he had to do was say he liked them. He tried them, didn't like them, and refused to endorse them. We now have about three offers in front of us, and I'm sure that he'll be able to do a good job for whatever sponsor he does anything for."

A quiet family man, McAdoo spent most of his free time at home with his young son Bob III and his wife Brenda, whom he met at the University of North Carolina. "He lived in a coed dorm," recalled Brenda. "One of the coeds there was my cousin Mitzi and she introduced him to me. On our first date, he didn't say much. After that he talked and kidded around. He isn't really quiet when he's around people he knows well."

McAdoo's off-court hobbies included photography and taking care of his Afghan hounds. "My female had nine puppies last summer," he said early in 1975. "I sold some of them but still have three back in Greensboro and two here in Buffalo." McAdoo also occasionally played the saxophone, a skill he developed while playing in bands from grade school through high school.

"We don't go out much here in Buffalo, and when we do, we catch a concert or a movie," said Brenda McAdoo. "I wouldn't mind living here all year round and it might help our future if we did, but Bob won't hear of it. He wants to build a house in Greensboro. When we're there for the off-season, we live with his parents, and he spends most of his spare time playing ball with his boyhood pals. That's when he's really happy. He's really comfortable with that bunch. And he is comfortable with his teammates

An exhausted McAdoo takes time out for a breather.

here. He does like to talk to sportswriters, but he feels that the out-of-town sportswriters ignore him. He'd like to talk to them because he can contribute."

He may have had trouble expressing himself at banquets and press conferences, but on a basketball court McAdoo said it all with a jump shot that spoke louder than words. Most great shooters made a study of their favorite shot. They learned the precise arc, release, and spin on the ball. Not Big Mac. Most great shooters had beautiful, graceful, textbook-perfect shots. Not Big Mac. All he ever did was line up the ball with the front of the rim and let fly with his strangely awkward-looking, herky-jerky jumper. But the scoreboard doesn't add points for looks.

"I don't think about the mechanics of the shot," Big Mac explained. "I just do what feels natural to me. I remember I was at a camp once when I was younger and Jerry West told me I had one of the ugliest shots he'd ever seen. He said he didn't know how the ball ever went in. Then he told me never to change my shot because the ball does go in. It was good advice. I have never changed it."

"It's hard to say exactly where I am in my development as a basketball player–I feel like I'm comparable to someone fourteen or fifteen years old."

Swen Nater

There's a special alarm that goes off in the brains of basketball coaches when they spot a potential star. It began clanging loudly inside the head of Cypress (California) Junior College assistant coach Tom Lubin the minute he saw the 6-foot-9 freshman ambling across the campus in the fall of 1968.

Lubin raced after the young giant, introduced himself, and fired off two quick questions: "What's your name and do you play basketball?"

"Swen Nater and no," replied the big kid.

That "no" triggered another automatic response peculiar to basketball coaches. Lubin was hit with an irresistible urge to teach the young giant the game. He just couldn't bear the thought of 81 inches of potential going to waste.

"How would you like to try it?" asked Lubin.

"Okay," replied Nater, whose only athletic experience up to that point had been a little soccer played as a boy in Del Helder, Holland, where he was born.

The scene shifts to the Cypress gym. Lubin stands in front of Nater, holds up a round brown sphere, and says, "This is a basketball." Swen Nater's education has begun.

By this time most young men of Nater's size—if they have any ability at all—have been playing basketball for years. The others profiled in this book were all outstanding high school players who were ardently wooed by scores of colleges.

Nater may have gotten a late start, but once he got going, his progress was amazingly fast. Just five years after his introduction to basketball, Nater was the starting center for the ABA Virginia Squires. And less than a year after that, he was named the league's Rookie of the Year.

Even Nater sometimes had trouble believing how far and how fast he'd come. "I'm still not caught up with guys who have been playing all their lives," he admitted after his outstanding rookie year. "They react to situations instinctively. I really have to concentrate when I'm playing and think things through. It's hard to say exactly where I am in my development as a basketball player. I feel like I'm comparable to someone fourteen or fifteen years old.

"I feel like I've come a long way—but, on the

other hand, I have a longer way to go. I'm learning every time we go out on the court. I've got a lot of catching up to do. I'd like to play twenty years of pro ball just to make up for not having played it before I did. And I would like to reach my maximum potential before I'm through."

If it hadn't been for coach Lubin, Nater might never have become a basketball player. But if it hadn't been for his stepfather, Nater might never have gotten to the United States and today might be the world's tallest soccer player.

Swen was six years old when his father, an accountant for the Dutch city of Hilversum, and his mother were divorced. Soon after, Swen's mother married a television salesman who wanted to emigrate to the United States. So when Swen was seven, his stepfather, mother, and five-year-old brother Ernie moved to Long Beach, California. Swen and his sister Nanna, 10, were left in a Dutch orphanage while their parents established themselves in their new homeland. "It was kind of frightening," said Swen, recalling his stay in the orphanage. "But my mother wrote us all the time, which helped a lot."

Two years later, Swen and his sister finally joined the rest of the family. Nater did not speak English when he arrived in California, but that was only a small part of the great adjustment he faced. "Yes, it was difficult at first," he admitted. "For one thing, back in Holland they think everyone in America is a cowboy running around on a horse and shooting a gun. I arrived in September and started school immediately. I made a big hit right away because I wore my guns and gunbelt to school the first day—and got laughed out of the class. If I had had a horse, I would have ridden him to school, too.

"Things were a lot different here. For example, in Holland all the boys wore short pants. Here they all wore long pants. Then there was the language difference. I got into a lot of fights at first. I got teased a lot."

Nater quickly learned to speak English, and he soon made friends. But it was years before he developed an interest in sports. "I was more into my studies," he explained.

Then, in his senior year of high school, Swen shot up four inches. The following fall, he enrolled at Cypress Junior College, where he was discovered by coach Lubin. "He worked with me day and night," Nater recalled. "It was a lot easier for me to start learning about basketball than it would have been for a smaller guy, but it still took a lot of work. I took about five hundred shots a day, plus working on my rebounding and defense.

"In my first year, I only played two or three minutes a game until the last two games of the season, which I started. That summer, I played ball every day, lifted weights, and put on about thirty pounds. I had a regular routine that my brother

Swen Nater was a latecomer to the world of basketball, but he quickly made up for lost time.

worked up for me, so when I went back to Cypress for my second year, I had improved a great deal."

In his second and final season at Cypress, Nater averaged 23 points and 18 rebounds per game, made the all-state junior college squad, and led his team to a 21–8 record. One of those victories was over the UCLA freshmen, a game in which Nater scored 23 points and grabbed 23 rebounds. "I guess John Wooden [the UCLA coach] was impressed," Nater said. "Anyway, I was offered a scholarship."

Wooden had long been considered a keen judge of talent. Over the years, he'd built a true dynasty at UCLA, and Bruin teams won a string of national championships under his direction. Nater, who was entering his junior year when he arrived at the UCLA campus some 70 miles north of Cypress in September 1970, was a fine prospect. But at the same time, Wooden had recruited an even better one, a 6-foot-11 high school star from La Mesa, California. His name was Bill Walton, and he had chosen UCLA from more than 100 college offers.

Obviously, only one big center could start for the Bruins, and it didn't take Nater any time at all to figure out which one it would be. When did Swen see the handwriting on the wall? "Immediately," he said with a grin.

But Walton wasn't all that stood between Nater and a starting spot on the team. Nater was just too inexperienced and undeveloped to play on a championship college team. Therefore, he chose to sit out his first year at UCLA so that he would not use up one of his two remaining years of eligibility. "Wooden left the choice up to me, but he made it clear I wouldn't play very much," Swen recalled. Walton, meanwhile, was leading the UCLA freshmen to an undefeated season, which included a victory over the defending national champions, the UCLA varsity.

The following year, Walton moved into the starting center position on the varsity. Nater moved to a seat on the bench—and that's where he remained for the next two seasons.

Practices at UCLA provided Nater with much of the experience against top competition he was not getting in games. "I got in a lot of good work," he said. "I always did well playing against Walton in practice. That's how I developed my hook shot. I had to use it. If you shoot a straight turnaround jump shot with Walton on you, the ball will be right back in your face. Against him I knew I had to shoot better, jump higher, and rebound better because I always knew he was going to be there. When you practice at your best all the time, it's got to make it easier in the game."

And whenever Walton was asked, which was often, he always said that the best center he ever faced in college was the one he played against in practice—Swen Nater.

If Nater resented playing second fiddle to Walton, he never showed it. "Walton's the greatest team-oriented player I've ever seen," he said. "Before each game he used to sit and just think and kind of get ready for the game by himself. We were good friends, but we didn't socialize off the court. Bill never socialized with anyone except Greg Lee. He's kind of a loner and I was, too."

As much as he respected Walton, it was coach Wooden who really inspired Nater. "It's the way he goes about doing something and the way he gets you to perform," explained Swen. "I don't know exactly what it is, but every guy on that team had so much respect for him and liked him so much they just wanted to break their necks to win for him.

"And one thing about his practices—the first was the same as the last. Fundamentals. Fundamentals. A couple of times I asked myself, 'We should have learned this by now, why don't we go on to something else?' But Wooden kept hammering it in until it became second nature. He said basketball is a game of quickness, and he wanted us to be able to react faster than our opponents. That's why going to practice at UCLA isn't that much different from playing in a game. The only fan is coach Wooden, but when you make a mistake he lets you know about it.

"Look at all the guys who have played for him. I think they are special people. They just seem to be

A second-stringer throughout his UCLA career, Nater makes a rare collegiate appearance in an exhibition game against a Soviet team.

able to handle life better. The players always looked at Wooden as a god. We called him St. John out of so much respect for him. You'd never talk back to him because he was like your father. You knew if you ever argued with him, there was another player just as good as you standing there and he would play the next night."

If he had it all to do over again, would Nater still attend UCLA? "Yes," he says, "because of the chance to play for coach Wooden."

Of course, Nater had some bad times at UCLA, too. A player with his potential confined to a career on the bench wouldn't have been human if he didn't get down in the dumps at least occasionally. "Sure, I got discouraged at times," he said. "Midway through my senior season I really got down on myself and quit trying. But Tom Lubin talked to me and I got my head together. I apologized to coach Wooden and told him it didn't matter if he played me or not, my attitude was going to change. Shortly after that, he put me at forward in a game against Cal and I started the second half, the only time I started at UCLA. We won by about twenty-five points, and I had my best game."

Nater's only other real chance to see some action had come just before that senior year. The 1972 Olympics were coming up, and the United States team trials were being held in June at the Air Force Academy in Colorado Springs, Colorado. Tendinitis kept Walton from trying out, so Nater finally got a chance to show the world what he could do. "That's all I want," he said upon arriving in Colorado, "just a chance to show myself. This is *me* now."

At the trials, Nater averaged 22 points and 10 rebounds per game to earn a place on the team. His new teammates kidded him about finally getting out of Walton's shadow and the number of shots he was taking now that Walton wasn't around to block them.

"I should be shooting well," Nater joked. "I had all winter to rest up."

Then he grew serious. "I guess this makes up for a lot of things," he said. "It's tough sitting on the bench all season. I tried not to let it get me down, though. On nights when I didn't play much, I used to come back to the gym after midnight and shoot. I guess it worked off a lot of nervous energy, if nothing else."

But Nater's long-awaited moment in the spotlight was not to be—at least not this time. After five days of practice at a submarine base in Honolulu, Hawaii, he quit the Olympic team. By then he had lost 20 pounds. The players were only allowed to eat twice a day—immediately after workouts—and Nater simply couldn't bring himself to eat at the prescribed times.

"We'd practice from about three to five o'clock," Nater recalled, "and we'd have to eat by five-thirty.

We were eating in the same mess hall with the sailors. The same thing at lunch. We'd practice from ten to twelve and have to eat by twelve-thirty.

"I asked the coach [Hank Iba] to arrange it so I could eat later. He said no. A lot of the players were complaining about the same thing—the meals coming so close to practice. The first day I got there I started to wonder about the whole situation. I tried to stick it out. Maybe I'd get used to it. Instead, I got weaker and weaker. I couldn't rebound. I couldn't do anything."

Although the food, or lack of it, was the reason he left, Nater also complained about the accommodations—old military barracks that he claimed were dirty and bug-infested. "But that was a side factor," Nater said. "I would have stayed there if I could have eaten properly. I don't think what I asked was too much. I would have overlooked the other conditions. But they shouldn't have been like that. After all, we were the U.S. Olympic team."

The rest of the U.S. players went on to Munich, Germany, where they lost the championship game to the Russians. Nater went back to UCLA and obscurity. That year, the Bruins won their seventh straight national championship, Walton was proclaimed All-Universe, and Nater ended his college career the way he began—applauding from his seat on the bench.

While he was at UCLA, Nater had devoted most

of his time and effort to basketball—at the expense of his studies. He switched his major from German to sociology to music and back to German. He finally left school without graduating—a failure Wooden sadly noted. "He said he was disappointed that I didn't graduate," Swen recalled. "I want to finish school, and I will."

Nater's biggest concern, however, was his future in pro basketball—which didn't look too certain because he had gotten so little exposure at UCLA. His varsity statistics—4.9 points and 4 rebounds per game—didn't help his case any. Fortunately, in April 1973, less than a month after the Bruins won their college title, Nater was invited to play in the Pizza Hut Classic in Las Vegas. It was his one and only college all-star game. He probably wouldn't have been invited to that one, either, had Walton been available. But Walton never showed any interest in participating in all-star games.

Nater realized that the professional scouts would attend in droves. "It was a do-or-die situation," he recalled. "No one really knew what I could do. Oh, they might have heard of me, but they were afraid to draft me high."

The day before the game, Steve Mitchell of Kansas State, the other center on the West team, injured his back in a workout. Nater, the man who hardly ever played, would have to go all the way without relief. Swen took full advantage of the opportunity. Firing hook shots and jumpers, rebounding, and playing tough defense, he was a real standout in a group that included some of the finest college players in the country. He put on a spectacular show, making 17 baskets in 26 attempts for 34 points. He also hauled down 23 rebounds.

Nater's performance was duly noted by the scouts, particularly the Milwaukee Bucks' general manager, Wayne Embry. In the 1973 NBA draft, Nater was Milwaukee's number one choice—but the Bucks weren't his first choice. Milwaukee already had an established center, a 7-foot-2 giant named Kareem Abdul-Jabbar, and Nater had had his fill of sitting behind a superstar. So Nater decided to sign with the Virginia Squires of the ABA. "If I'd gone to Milwaukee, it would have been more of the same," he explained.

All rookies face big adjustments when they enter professional ball. Because of his unusually limited college background, Nater had a tougher time than most. "First of all, I had to adjust to playing," he said. "I wasn't used to actually playing in games that matter under pressure situations. It wasn't a matter of getting tired or anything like that. That's just physical conditioning. I simply hadn't played in many games that counted.

"More specifically, I had to work hardest on my defense. I had to learn to use a lot more body contact. If I had played in college the way I play in

A rookie with the Virginia Squires in 1973, Nater has trouble guarding Kentucky's Artis Gilmore.

the pros, I would have fouled out in five minutes. I had to learn to block shots. When a teammate gets beat on defense, you have to be ready to jump in there and stop his man before he gets the easy bucket. You know, a center will block a lot more shots on somebody else's men than he will on his own man. And a good center has to block shots."

Rebounding was one thing Nater did well right from the start. By his rookie year, he had shot up to 6-foot-11 and weighed 250 pounds. "Aside from size, which is obvious, positioning is the key to good rebounding," he said. "Then there's desire and timing and learning to protect the ball once you've got it. But positioning is the key. Look at Jerry Lucas [the former NBA star]. He wasn't tremendous, and he certainly wasn't a great leaper, but he was a great rebounder because of the way he consistently got good position."

A big man who rebounds and defends well is the heart of any pro team. The Squires knew right away that once the rough edges were polished, they would have a winner in Nater, a man they might build a whole team around. And Nater was just as impressed with the Squires. He made friends easily and quickly and was popular with teammates and fans alike. Therefore, Nater and all the Squires were shocked and disappointed when the big rookie was traded to the San Antonio Spurs a few months after the 1973–74 season began. "I was down, very depressed when I learned about it," he said. "I had let my roots sink deeply in Virginia and the thought of leaving friends there hurt. I knew the fans, and the fans knew me. It was a good situation, and I really was enjoying myself. We were a family. I thought I'd be in Norfolk for ten or twelve years."

The reason for the trade was no secret. Squires owner Earl Foreman was in desperate financial trouble. In an effort to keep his franchise, he was selling his top players for cash. Virginia had already given up such superstars as Julius Erving, Rick Barry, Charlie Scott, and George Gervin.

It cost San Antonio $300,000 plus a high draft choice to get Nater—but he was worth every bit of it. "You need a big strong guy at center if you expect to contend," said Spurs coach Tom Nissalke. "Swen has given us a new dimension inside. We were strictly a high post team without him. But now we can use the low post. And there's no way you can ever be a winner if you can't go in low.

"People thought Bill Walton was joking when he said the best big man he played against in college was Swen during practice at UCLA. They are going to learn that Walton was telling the truth."

Nater got off to a fine start with the Spurs and was chosen for the ABA's All-Star West team. The game was played on January 31, 1974, in—of all places— the Norfolk home of the Squires. Nater showed the Virginians what they'd given up—and that was plenty. He set All-Star records for most two-point field goals attempted (24), most made (13), most rebounds (22), and most offensive rebounds (13). His 29 points were one short of tying a fifth record.

Unfortunately, Nater's great effort came in a losing cause. Largely because he was on the winning East team, Kentucky's 7-foot-2 center, Artis Gilmore (who scored 18 points and had 13 rebounds), was voted the game's Most Valuable Player. When the award was announced, the 10,624 packed into the arena booed loudly, indicating their displeasure with the decision and showing their continuing affection for Nater.

Some players also questioned the selection of Gilmore. "How could they help but give Nater the award?" demanded Rich Jones of the Spurs. "He's my *most* MVP."

Only Nater himself refused to quarrel with the choice. "I just wanted the West to win," he said. "I didn't even know there was a trophy until I saw it. Now that I did, I'm glad I didn't win. The thing is too big to carry. Me MVP? Heck, I'm in a daze just being here."

One reason Nater wasn't too disappointed at losing the award to Gilmore was his great respect for the huge Colonel pivotman. When asked who was the hardest man in the league for him to guard, Swen replied in one word: "Artis."

"He's the toughest because he's so big," Nater

Nater and Gilmore meet again in the 1974 ABA All-Star Game, and this time Swen comes out on top.

explained. "He likes to go into the basket to shoot. I've got to try to make him set up two or three feet further out than he'd like so he has to take an extra dribble to get in. Then you hope they call a charging foul or someone steals the ball.

"Billy Paultz of the Nets is also tough because he can hit that open 15-footer. You're trying to help out by picking up a teammate's man, and he flips it out to Paultz for the open shot. He hits them.

"San Diego's Caldwell Jones is a problem because he's a good shot-blocker. He makes you choose your shots more carefully. Marvin Barnes is coming along in St. Louis, Denver's Mike Green is a heckuva shooter . . . they're all tough."

But no one was any tougher than Nater, particularly after he'd given himself a good pre-game peptalk. "You've got to get up for the game," he explained, "and that becomes a problem when you play so many of them. I talk to myself a lot, reminding myself what I have to do. You can't go into a game just saying, 'I've got to play well,' or at least I can't. I have to break it down, thinking about who I'm playing, what he likes to do, and so forth. That kind of gets the adrenalin going.

"Then during a game, I first think about rebounding. If I have a good rebounding game, we generally win. I also look to score eighteen points or so and block around four shots."

Nater did even better than that in one 1974 game

Playing for the San Antonio Spurs in '74, Nater is fouled in the act of shooting.

against the championship-bound New York Nets. That night he scored 22 points and grabbed 26 rebounds. "It's somewhat surprising that he's come along so fast," said Net general manager Dave DeBusschere. "He hasn't had much game competition. He's never really had the pressure on him that you have in the game. It's nice and all that he played against Bill Walton in practice, but that's not the same thing."

Nater finished his first season with a league-leading field-goal percentage of 55.3, scored 14.1 points per game, and averaged 12.6 rebounds, fourth best in the ABA. He used his brawny body with great effectiveness on defense. The Spurs finished their season in good shape, too. Before they obtained Nater, the Spurs had an 11–12 record. But with the big man in the pivot, they'd wound up with a 45–39 mark, an improvement of seven games.

It's not surprising that Nater was voted Rookie of the Year, although there were several other super-rookies that season. Swen received 24 first-place votes to 23 for teammate Caldwell Jones and 13 for New York Net forward Larry Kenon. "It's really a surprise," Nater said upon learning of the honor. "After the All-Star game, I admit I started thinking about it, but then I shoved it into the back of my mind because my major concern was making the playoffs.

"Yes, there is a lot of personal satisfaction. It was

just not playing all those years while knowing you can play that bothers you. To win this honor, it's like taking a chain off."

Swen Nater was finally out of Bill Walton's shadow for good.

"I've watched them all in this league for seven years," said Virginia veteran Cincy Powell shortly after Nater's award. "I've watched the league grow. First our guards could match those in the NBA, then our forwards could more than match theirs. And now our young centers, well, they can hold their own. Swen can become one of the best, maybe the very best. He has all the tools. He's strong and he can jump. He's intelligent and he can shoot. He won't take a lot of shoving around, either."

Nater's second pro season (1974–75) was as impressive as his first. This time, he wound up with 15.1 points and a league-leading 16.4 rebounds.

As a rookie, Nater had said that because of his late start in the game he felt comparable to a player 14 or 15 years old. After his excellent sophomore season, he was asked if he felt he had grown up any.

Nater thought for a moment, smiled and said, "Going on eighteen."

"It's not my job to look good. It's my job to make other people look good."

Wes Unseld

Capital Centre, October 26, 1974. The Washington Bullets have the ball and are passing it around in an attempt to get off a good shot against the visiting Milwaukee Bucks. Ten players are in motion, sneakers squeaking and bodies soaked with perspiration. The ball flies from Bullet to Bullet with the Bucks in hot pursuit.

Washington guard Phil Chenier dribbles toward the right corner and drops the ball off to forward Mike Riordan. Closely guarded, Riordan fires the ball out to guard Kevin Porter, who immediately bounces a pass to forward Elvin Hayes in the other corner. The movement of the ball is quick, smooth, and fluid—but so is the Bucks' defense. Now time is running out on the shooting clock. The Bullets must put the ball up soon or lose it on a 24-second violation.

Suddenly, Washington center Wes Unseld, a tree of a man at 6-foot-7 and 245 pounds, moves out to a spot near the top of the key. He forces his huge body between the dribbling Chenier and Chenier's defender, Milwaukee guard Jim Price. Price shoves and pushes Unseld in a desperate effort to stay close to Chenier, but he might as well be trying to move a mountain. Unseld doesn't budge. Given a clear shot at the basket, Chenier leaps high in the air and gracefully swishes the ball through the net. The home crowd applauds Chenier's classic jump shot.

The Bucks take the ball out and move slowly upcourt. Milwaukee super-center Kareem Abdul-Jabbar lopes into the forecourt and sets up on the left side of the foul lane with his back to the basket. He calls for the ball by raising one huge hand. Unseld is almost lost behind the 7-foot-2 Buck.

Milwaukee guard Gary Brokaw floats a lob pass to Kareem, who immediately tries to back in closer to the basket. But Unseld is in his way. As Abdul-Jabbar dribbles right, Wes keeps his thick body glued to him, forcing him away from the basket. Kareem takes a final giant step and goes up for one of his awesome skyhooks, a sweeping hook shot he actually fires *down* into the basket. No one alive can block that shot. When Abdul-Jabbar releases it from his favorite spot on the floor, he hardly ever misses.

Wes Unseld gets set to heave one of his patented outlet passes against the Milwaukee Bucks.

But this time (thanks to Unseld), the Milwaukee center is just a little further away from the hoop than he likes. The ball bounces off the front rim. With a speed belying his great bulk, Wes snaps up the rebound. Before his feet have even hit the ground, he fires it half the length of the court to Porter, who had taken off the other way as soon as Kareem took the shot. Streaking upcourt on the other side is Chenier. Both Bullet guards have anticipated Unseld's rebound.

The only Buck defender back is Brokaw, who crouches in the middle under the basket as the two speeding Bullets approach. Porter dribbles in and begins to go up for a lay-up. Brokaw leaps to block the shot, so Porter bounces the ball to Chenier. Chenier drops in an easy lay-up. The home crowd applauds Porter's beautifully timed pass.

Unseld falls back to his defensive position. The fans ignore him. Like most basketball spectators, they've been following the ball. Therefore, they never even noticed the pick or screen that set up Chenier's jump shot, the unyielding defense against Abdul-Jabbar that forced the feared skyhook into a rare misfire, or the ensuing rebound and lightning-quick outlet pass that led to the Bullets' fast-break lay-up. But that didn't bother Unseld. *He* knew he had done his job, and he knew the other players and coaches knew it, too.

"It's not my job to look good," Unseld once

explained. "It's my job to make other people look good."

Coaches have always stressed the importance of unselfishness and team play, but very few professional athletes have ever displayed those virtues as consistently as Wes Unseld. He made his contribution by doing basketball's dirty work and left the scoring and headlines to others. Unseld may have been underrated by the public, but his teammates certainly appreciated his true value.

"He doesn't even think about scoring," said Bullet forward Mike Riordan. "Most players, when they get the ball, instinctively look for a shot. Wes instinctively looks for the open man. Totally unselfish. He keeps the ball moving so much that everybody gets a piece of the action. Guys love playing with him. He makes everybody else look good. I guess that's why he never gets any publicity. Most people are impressed by scoring statistics. The players are more impressed by all the other things he does, his ability to neutralize other people."

"He can play," said Kevin Loughery, the Bullet guard who later went on to coach the ABA New York Nets. "He's so strong—and so quick. He gets the ball out on the break, and he moves much better with the ball than I thought he would. When he goes to the basket, he gets there. It's that simple. He's almost impossible to stop because he's so strong he doesn't lose control of the ball."

"I have to admit I didn't know just how great he really was when I came here," said Bullet coach K. C. Jones. "You have to be with him to appreciate how much he does. It's that air of leadership. He just does it all. He's so big, yet so quick."

In fact, the only Bullet who didn't rave about the big center was Unseld, himself. "On the teams I've played on as a pro, nobody has paid to see me play," Wes explained. "They paid to see Earl Monroe and Gus Johnson when they were on the team, and now they pay to see Chenier and Elvin Hayes. My style simply isn't flashy—on or off the court. Lack of publicity doesn't bother me. In fact, publicity annoys me. It's embarrassing. It's embarrassing to talk about yourself, and it's embarrassing to think that somebody would want to read about me. This hero worship stuff is wrong. The kids should be looking up to someone who's doing something important."

Wes was as unselfish and modest off the court as he was on it. When the Bullets were playing in Baltimore before their move to Washington, the sponsors of the Neighborhood Basketball League wanted a Bullet to serve as a figurehead commissioner. Jim Henneman, who was then team public relations director, suggested Unseld. "But I told them Unseld wouldn't be a figurehead, that he'd really work at it, that he'd want to get involved," Henneman recalled. "Unseld was capable of commanding two or three hundred dollars a day at summer clinics or camps and he could have made a thousand dollars a week in the Catskills. Instead, he chose to spend three years at a nonpaying job because he felt his presence would have an effect. I like to think he touched some of those kids. It's pretty hard to be exposed to him and not have a little of his class rub off."

That class was apparent from the time Unseld first went to Baltimore as a rookie in June 1968 and began making appearances at playgrounds and clinics. "We often get a thank-you note when one of our players makes an appearance," Henneman said, "but you should have seen the letters we got when Westley appeared. He really made an impression. He said he loved to meet people, and they really like him."

Unseld also made numerous visits to the Kernan Hospital for Crippled Children in Baltimore, where the patients came to affectionately call him "The Jolly Green Giant." Although he received several awards from local civic groups for his contributions to the community, Unseld tried to play down his volunteer work.

"I get a great deal of satisfaction out of it, but it's something that has become completely overblown and overpublicized," he said during the 1974–75 season.

"I don't do that much now that I'm married and have a daughter. When I was a bachelor, I had time

An intense Unseld watches his Washington teammates from the bench.

on my hands, so this type of activity gave me a chance to get out and meet people as well as do some good. But it's nothing to make a big deal over."

Wes learned about unselfishness early in life from his parents. Mr. and Mrs. Charles Unseld of Louisville, Kentucky, had five sons and two daughters. All seven went to college, despite the fact that their father, a construction worker, was far from a wealthy man. Wes, the second oldest son, recalled, "My parents used to say to me, 'There's only one way for a Negro to get ahead these days, and that's by going to college.' It became a little easier when we boys started winning scholarships, but my father worked two jobs to put my two sisters through school at almost the same time. He got himself a couple of heart attacks, but he made sure we got through. My father really sacrificed for us. He's a pretty good old man.

"He has probably been the strongest influence on my life. The one thing he used to point out all the time was the value of learning how to work, no matter what type of work it was. Just do your job well—that's what he taught us."

The senior Unselds expected their children to stay out of trouble. Wes learned that when he was still in grade school. "I remember my mother saying, 'If you ever get in trouble, I'll come over there and whip you in front of the whole school,' " he recalled with a smile. "I never gave her the opportunity, but she'd probably do that now, too, if I messed up."

Although his family did have financial problems, Wes was never aware of them. "I didn't know about being poor," he explained. "It just seemed normal to me. I had a happy childhood. No problems, no worries. I was always doing something. I had to make my own fun—that is, when I wasn't helping my father. It was hard work, lifting and mixing mortar and things like that."

Wes even found a way to get some fun out of his work. When he was ten years old, he built his own barbells. "I took a sack of my father's concrete and two big mason jars," he explained. "I filled the jars with concrete and stuck a pipe in between them into the necks. I let the concrete harden, broke the glass on the jars, and—presto!—I had my first pair of barbells."

It was about that time that Wes discovered basketball. "I was walking past the playground one day when my fifth-grade teacher grabbed me," Wes recalled. "She said we were playing the sixth-grade team and that she needed a replacement for the center who hadn't shown up. She forced me to play.

"Well, I was just awful. I was clumsy and unsure of myself. I couldn't dribble the ball at all. I was so disgusted, I didn't pick up a basketball again for four years."

Wes finally gave the game another try when his older brother George became a great success at Seneca High School. George Unseld, 6-foot-8 and

235 pounds at maturity, was a high school All-America who went on to star at the University of Kansas. "I just couldn't believe how good my brother was at the game," Wes said. "I lived with the guy, and he just didn't look that good to me to be an All-America. I said to myself, 'If he can be an All-America, there's no telling what I could be.'"

Wes soon found out that basketball stardom didn't come easy. He tried out for his eighth-grade team and was cut. What's more, his younger brother Reggie, then in the sixth grade, made the team. "That really burned me up," Wes admitted. "I decided I was through with the game for good."

Wrong again. As a freshman at Seneca High, Wes watched brother George get royal-carpet treatment from dozens of college recruiters. "People were coming around all the time wooing him, trying to make him come to their school," Wes recalled. "He was always taking trips and things. I thought, 'Hmmmm, I'd like some of that, too.'"

Encouraged by Seneca High coach Carl Wright, who apparently saw a diamond in the rough, Wes tried out for the team. "Mr. Wright could just about leap over tall buildings," Wes said, "and he had a build like Tarzan. I figured that if he got that way playing basketball, I ought to give it more time."

This time Wes succeeded. He led the Seneca freshmen in scoring and rebounding. Then over the summer he shot up four and one-half inches and filled out to become a burly 6-foot-5 sophomore center on the varsity. Mr. Wright now looked small next to Unseld.

Although Wes was a starter as a sophomore, he was overshadowed by the team's returning veterans. In his junior year, however, he did everything a player should—except score a lot of points. His unselfish contributions led Seneca to the state championship, and Wes made the all-state team. More important, he learned the basic philosophy of basketball that he would later follow as a pro.

"I don't want to sound like I'm bragging," Unseld said of his first two varsity seasons, "but I was always taught that anybody can score twenty points in a game if he shoots enough. But my coaches always asked me how many guys can grab twenty rebounds a game.

"Besides, there was no reason for me to shoot. We had a couple of All-Americas on those teams who could really fill the hoop. To play on those teams, you had to do something special to impress the coach. So I just started concentrating on perfecting my rebounding, defense, and other aspects of the game. I couldn't think of anything else to do. I got the ball and let our two hotshot guards do the shooting."

As a senior, Wes was the only returning regular. The high-scoring guards had graduated, so he had to assume greater shooting responsibility. And he did,

Playing for Seneca High in 1964, Wes appears to have a basketball for a head as he pulls down a rebound.

more than doubling his average from 12.1 to 24.5 points per game. In addition, he averaged 21 rebounds a game. Seneca became the first team in 30 years to repeat as Kentucky state champion. Wes headed the all-state team, made most high school All-America squads, and was swamped with more than 100 college scholarship offers.

Unseld's ability and character were so highly regarded that several Southeastern Conference schools, including the University of Kentucky, wanted him to become the league's first black player. But Unseld was not interested. "I told my mother then that if I played in the SEC I'd set civil rights back twenty years," he explained years later. "A lot of people felt I should be the first black to play. I told them I didn't have the right attitude to be a pioneer—that it just wasn't me. I have the same attitude now. I feel if someone is nice to me, then I'll be nice to them. But if someone isn't nice, well, I believe in talking to them in a language that they will understand. If a man spits on me, I'll probably spit back. Feeling like that, I didn't think I'd make a very good barrier-breaker."

Wes finally decided to stay home and attend the University of Louisville. "The biggest reason was that my father had just had his second heart attack," he explained. "I remember how it seemed like he saved forever to buy one of those eight- or ten-band radios so he could pick up my brother's games in

Kansas. It really hurt him that he couldn't watch George play. My father was the type that not only came to every game in high school, but also to every practice. I felt like I should go somewhere where he could at least see me play."

At Louisville, Wes put on quite a show for his father and the fans. He averaged 35.8 points and 23.6 rebounds per game, leading the freshman team to a perfect 15–0 record. The following year, he was second in the country in rebounding with 19.4 per game, was named Sophomore of the Year in the Missouri Valley Conference, and was a unanimous all-conference selection. As a junior and senior, he made almost all the important All-America teams. In his three varsity years, Unseld averaged 20.6 points and 18.9 rebounds per game, and Louisville racked up a sparkling 60–22 record.

But there was more to college than basketball for Unseld. "I always think of the beginning of my junior year as the time I matured as a person," he said. "I just decided I wanted an education and I was going to work hard at getting it.

"You know, I played ball in high school with a bunch of guys who were All-Americas. The playground clowns used to say that except for my brother, none of us who made All-America and got scholarships to college ever finished school. When one of us dropped out, they would say, 'One down, three to go,' and cracks like that. That's what made me determined to graduate. I had never taken school terribly seriously before because I never had any problems getting good grades. But just getting by, even if your grades are good, is not really getting an education."

Despite his outstanding basketball credentials, Unseld was not counting on a professional career. "You have to realize that in Louisville we weren't that familiar with pro ball," Wes explained. "The ABA was new in town, and before that all we ever saw was the Sunday game of the week on television. And my brother George had turned the pros down. I know he could have been a good pro. I don't have any doubts about that at all. He's a better ballplayer than me. He's smarter about the game than me. When I have a problem now, I still call him up for advice. But he just didn't want to play pro ball. He's the type of person who makes up his own mind. He just won't do anything he doesn't think is right for him. He preferred to go into teaching."

Wes knew he wanted to play pro ball, but he wasn't at all sure that the pros wanted him. Then in the middle of his senior year (Christmas Day 1967) he got his first offer—from the ABA's Kentucky Colonels, who were playing their first season in Louisville. The Colonels offered Unseld a reported $500,000 and took out an ad in a Louisville paper imploring him to play pro ball in front of his hometown fans. But Wes rejected the Colonels and signed with the NBA Baltimore Bullets for half the money.

"The only reason I went with the Bullets was that the Colonels did something that turned my father against them," he explained. "I prefer not to say what it was. The money? Sure, it was important, but I had my degree and I figured I could always make a living. You never miss money if you've never had it, so I didn't lose any sleep over it."

Ironically, the Bullets weren't nearly as enthusiastic about Unseld as the Colonels had been. Baltimore coach Gene Shue had scouted Unseld at the end of Wes' sophomore year and had not been particularly impressed with him. "Unseld's an odd size and awfully small to play the pivot," Shue said at the time. "His speed is horrible, although he does have real good quickness. His shooting also must be considered questionable."

The man whom Shue and the Bullets really wanted was Elvin Hayes of the University of Houston. But the San Diego Rockets (who later moved to Houston) had the first pick in the 1968 draft—and they selected Hayes. So Baltimore had to "settle" for Unseld.

The Bullets never regretted signing Unseld. He proved from the start that he had a great deal to contribute to the team. The long schedule, the constant travel, and the far more physical game played by the pros are often most difficult for rookies

As a Bullet rookie in 1968, Unseld shows his strength under the boards.

to adjust to. But they were a breeze for Unseld. "The easiest part for me was the physical aspect," he says. "We played a pretty physical brand of ball in the Missouri Valley Conference and that was my kind of game, anyway. And I enjoyed the travel in my rookie year—moving around, seeing the sights and all. I don't think I ever got tired."

Unseld proved remarkably poised and mature for a rookie. "Actually, you didn't think of him as a rookie," said coach Shue (who later went on to coach the Philadelphia Seventy-Sixers). "He acted like he'd been around for years. His college coach, John Dromo, said that Westley had a keen mind for the game. We found out right away that was true."

Bob Ferry, an assistant coach who sometimes came in as Unseld's replacement at center, put it this way: "I call Wes 'the Computer.' That's because as soon as you tell him something, he does it. You don't have to wonder if it will happen, or if he will mess it up, or if he'll feel like doing it. No, he just does it. And he does it right every time. Things that took me ten years to learn to do, Wes can do now—because he has much quicker reactions than I did."

San Francisco (now Golden State) Warrior guard Jeff Mullins said, "I don't believe the Bullets would have been as well off if they had won the flip and grabbed Hayes. They already had great shooters like Earl Monroe, Kevin Loughery, Jack Marin, and Gus

Johnson. They didn't need another big scorer like Hayes.

"With Hayes, they might still have been a collection of individuals with ability. But with Unseld, they became a team. He is so unselfish that all he cares about is getting the ball off the boards and passing it out to one of his teammates." (Hayes eventually became one of those teammates in 1972-73 when the Bullets acquired him from the Rockets and gave up Jack Marin).

The bottom line on any athlete is how much he helps his team. The year before Unself joined them, the Bullets had finished last in the Eastern Division with a 36-46 record. With Unseld in 1968-69 they finished first with a 57-25 mark, an astounding improvement of 21 games. Atlanta Hawks coach Richie Guerin simply shook his head and said, "It's hard to believe that one guy could make such a difference in a team."

Although Wes averaged only 13.8 points per game in his first season, he finished second in the league in rebounding with 18.2 per game and did all the unglamorous—but essential—things that never show up in a boxscore. At the end of his memorable rookie season, he became the second man in NBA history to be named Rookie of the Year and Most Valuable Player in the same year (Wilt Chamberlain was the first). His 53 first-place votes in the players' MVP balloting were more than the next four finishers got combined. Wes' reaction to that honor was typically low key. "Know where I was when I heard about it?" he asked with a smile. "Out fishing. I thought, 'Hey, well, that's okay. It's a nice trophy.'"

For the next four seasons, Unseld was a model of consistency. He averaged 16.2, 14.1, 13.0, and 12.5 points per game, grabbed 16.7, 16.9, 17.8, and 15.9 rebounds, played his tenacious defense, set picks, pitched out, moved the ball, and in his own words "made other people look good." In his first five years as a pro he missed only 17 regular-season games out of 410. He was the rock the Bullets relied on.

The height disadvantage that Shue once worried about proved harmless. "The only problem it creates is that I never have an easy night," Wes explained. "When I play somebody six-foot-ten or seven feet tall, it means I automatically have to work a little bit harder than he does. He's coming in with a natural advantage. He can go at his medium pace, but I have to go at my maximum to keep up."

Going at his maximum night after night, season after season, finally took its toll during the 1973–74 season. Unseld's left knee, which had given him periodic problems since his college days, gave way, and he limped through a miserable, pain-racked year. Many people, including Wes, began to wonder if his career had reached a tragically premature end. That year he played in only 56 of 82 games, often making only token appearances. He hardly ever practiced. Before one game, 200 cubic centimeters (almost a cup) of fluid was drained from his knee. He lost his mobility. He couldn't jump. His scoring average dropped to 5.9 points per game and his rebounds to 9.2. He knew he needed an operation, but even with surgery there were no guarantees that he would ever be able to play his old rough and ready style of ball again.

"I knew my career might be over, but I didn't get terribly depressed about it," he said later. "It's something that's going to happen to all of us one day. I just thought my time might have come sooner than the next guy's. I like to think I was realistic about it."

In May 1974 Wes underwent surgery. Cartilage was removed from the knee, bone spurs were scraped away, and the kneecap was reset. Unseld spent the next few months rebuilding strength in the knee, but until he got back into competition, he couldn't be sure it would hold up. "I've got a fear," he admitted right before the start of the 1974–75 season. "I don't want to overdo it. I'm scared of getting hurt again."

After a seemingly endless summer of waiting, Unseld finally got to test the rebuilt knee under combat conditions. It wasn't perfect—it never again would be—but it was good enough. "Some nights the knee is fine, almost as good as it ever was," he said early in 1975. "But most of the time I know it's

Unseld makes a valiant effort to stop Kareem Abdul-Jabbar, but the big Buck stuffs the ball through the hoop.

there, and some nights it gives me problems. It fills up with fluids and becomes hard to bend. But I think I still manage to do the job."

Unseld did the job to the tune of a league-leading 14.8 rebounds per game. He also scored 9.2 points per game.

But as usual, the numbers hardly described his contribution to the team. The Bullets finished the season with a 60–22 record, tops in their division. Most fans, even those who consider themselves basketball experts, probably have no idea exactly how much the Westley Unselds of the game actually do out on the court. Everyone's too busy following the ball. Asked to talk about his responsibilities, Wes laughed and said, "It sounds dumb, but the first thing I have to do is get the ball out of bounds and back into play quickly after the other team scores. That gets the ball down the floor quickly and always keeps their defense on the defensive. It doesn't give them a chance to rest or set up. It keeps constant pressure on them.

"Then I have to set picks. There's no secret to it. All you have to do is get your body between where the offensive man wants to go and the defensive man wants to get. The reason some guys do it better than others is probably because some guys have a higher pain threshold. Picks hurt. It's that simple. If they didn't, everybody would be setting them. The guys trying to get by you are not usually very fussy about how they do it."

Unseld also stressed the importance of making strong outlet passes. "The only reason I think I do it better than some other guys is that I want to do it and they don't seem to think too much about it," he said. "There's no real knack to it. It can be done by anybody. I really don't know why other players don't do it. It certainly has helped us."

Picks and passes certainly helped, but by far Unseld's most important contribution to the Bullets was his defense. "One important thing on defense is not to become just a shot-blocker," he explained. "Now there's nothing wrong with blocking shots, but I've seen guys who became shot-blockers and just stopped there. And that's not all there is to playing defense. Far from it.

"In my philosophy of defense, you actually have to play the man. All the time. The way I look at it is that you're not going to stop a man every time, but you can try to always put him in an unfavorable scoring position by taking away something that he likes to do. To do that, though, you obviously have to first know what he likes to do. That's the most important thing in playing defense, I think. You have to know if he likes to drive, if he likes to fake, if he's right-handed, if he's left-handed. I scout my opponents just as carefully as any baseball or football player does. It's the key to playing good defense."

Here's Wes Unseld's scouting report on some of the NBA's top centers:

"Bob Lanier is difficult to play because he can go outside on you. He's a terrific shooter for a big man, and he's left-handed, which creates a problem in defending against him. You're used to going against guys who are right-handed, so when you face a lefty it makes you stop and think, which sometimes makes you hesitate. It's unnatural. I know that Lanier wants to go left, so I try to play up on that left hand of his and force him to go to his right.

"Dave Cowens is a big threat to drive. He's also a left-hander. So I try to play up on his left hand and force him right, and I guard against the drive. He really runs around a lot out there, which I understand gives some guys trouble. But it doesn't bother me. The court's not that long.

"Bob McAdoo is more of a problem than any of them, because you never know exactly what he's going to do out there, at least I don't. He moves around all the time trying to get the ball. Most of the other centers look to dish the ball out to their teammates, but Bob looks to get it dished to him, which makes him harder to guard. I know what he wants to do when he gets the ball. He wants to take two or three dribbles to his left and go up with that jump shot. He always wants to go left, so I try to force him right.

Wes gets tangled up with Boston's Paul Silas, but still manages to hold on to the ball.

"Jabbar is Jabbar, the one and only. He's not tough to play in the sense that you don't know what he's going to do. He wants to come down, line up on that left side, and come across with that right-handed hook. The problem is, how do you stop it? All you can do is try to throw off his rhythm or get him a step further out than he wants to be. You can't really muscle him very effectively. Lots of people don't realize that Jabbar is quite strong."

Going one-on-one against basketball's biggest men, game after game, season after season, was a difficult job. Add exhibitions and playoff games to the 82 regular-season contests, and the total comes to over 100 games every year. That adds up to thousands of picks, thousands of collisions, thousands of races up and down the court, hundreds of plane rides, and countless hours in hotels. The grind takes a psychological as well as a physical toll. After seven years in the league, Unseld often felt the strain.

"At this stage, I really don't know if I enjoy playing basketball that much," Unseld admitted midway through the 1974–75 season. "It became work to me quite a while ago. I enjoy doing it rather than doing some other type of work, but as for getting a kick out of playing ball . . . not any more. I've had my share of injuries, and I think it's hard to maintain a great deal of enthusiasm for anything if you've been doing it long enough."

Off the court, Wes relaxed by fishing for bass,

taking and developing photographs, going to the movies or theater, or staying home with his wife and daughter. After he's through with basketball? "If you had asked me that before I had the knee operation, I could have told you ten things I was interested in doing," he said. "Now I'm not so sure. One possibility would be going back to school and working toward a physical therapy certificate. That's something I've become interested in and enjoy."

If Unseld does go into physical therapy work, you can bet he'll be good at it. A long time ago, Charles Unseld taught his sons how important it is for them to do their job well—and it was a lesson Wes Unseld would never forget.

Index

Page numbers in italics refer to photographs.

Abdul-Jabbar, Kareem, 25, 31, 52, 58, 60, 71, 72, 87, 88, *89*, 120, *141*, 146
Alexander, Lonnie, 15, 16
Atlanta Hawks, 49, 50
Auerbach, Red, 42, 49, 52, 56
Awtrey, Dennis, 33

Baltimore Bullets, 55
 see also Washington Bullets
Barnes, Marvin, 114
Barry, Rick, 111
Ben L. Smith High School, 69, 75
Bennett High School, 16
Bing, Aaris, 26, 28
Bing, Dave, 13, 25, 26, *27*, 28, 29, 33
Boston Celtics, 9, 37–46, 49–67
Bradley, Bill, 80
Bridges, Bill, 71

Brokaw, Gary, 120, 122
Buffalo Braves, 13, 70–75, 79–93
Buntin, Bill, 80

Capital Center (Washington D.C.), 119
Carolina Cougars, 79
Catholic High School, 46
Chamberlain, Wilt, 138
Chaney, Don, 57
Chenier, Phil, 119, 120, 122, 124
Cobo Arena (Detroit), 9, 10
Conlin, Bill, 18
Connor, Jim, 47
Cowens, Dave, 31, 33, 37–67, 72, 144
 college career, 47–49
 early life, 46–47
 photos of, *35*, *39*, *45*, *51*, *54*, *59*, *61*, *66*

with Boston Celtics, 37–46, 49–67
Cypress Junior College, 95

Davis, Mel, 87
DeBusschere, Dave, 85, 116
Detroit Pistons, 9–15, 20–35, 49
DiGregorio, Ernie, 84
Donovan, Eddie, 80
Dromo, John, 137
Durham, Hugh, 47, 48

Erving, Julius, 111

Ferry, Bob, 137
Finkel, Henry, 43, 55
Florida State University, 47–49
Ford, Curtis, 18
Foreman, Earl, 111
Frazier, Walt, 59, 87

Gervin, George, 111
Gianelli, John, 86
Gilmore, Artis, 48, 109, 112, 113
Gold, Phyliss, 64
Gold, Richard, 64
Green, Mike, 114
Goukas, Matt, 84
Guerin, Richie, 138

Hairston, Happy, 54
Havlicek, John, 40, 57, 58
Hawkins, Connie, 23
Hayes, Elvin, 119, 124, 135
Haywood, Spencer, 30, 72
Heard, Garfield, 45, 84
Heinsohn, Tom, 38, 40, 49, 53, 55, 57
Henneman, Jim, 124, 125

Holzman, Red, 44
Houston Rockets, 84
Hudson, Lou, 80

Jacksonville, University of, 48
Johnson, Gus, 55, 124, 138
Jones, Caldwell, 114, 116
Jones, K.C., 124
Jones, Rich, 112

Kansas, University of, 129
Kauffman, Bob, 84
Kenon, Larry, 116
Kentucky, University of, 132
Kentucky Colonels, 134
King, George, 17

Lacey, Sam, 31, 33
Lanier, Bob, 9–35, 49, 71, 88, 144
  college career, 17–20
  early life, 15–17
  photos of, 11, 12, 19, 23, 27, 32, 83
  with Detroit Pistons, 9–15, 20–35
Lanier, Shirley Neville, 26, 30
Lee, Greg, 102
Lotz, John, 76
Loughery, Kevin, 123, 137
Louisville, University of, 132
Lubin, Tom, 95, 96, 97, 98, 104
Lucas, Jerry, 110

Madden, Bill, 90
Madison Square Garden (New York), 17, 37
Maravich, Pete, 49, 50
Marin, Jack, 84, 137
Marlatt, Harvey, 20
Martzke, Rudy, 81

INDEX

McAdoo, Bob, 31, 69–93, 144
   college career, 76–79
   early life, 75–76
   photos of, *67, 73, 78, 83, 86, 89, 92*
   with Boston Braves, 70–75, 79–93
McAdoo, Brenda, 91
McMillian, Jim, 82
Miller, Larry, 80
Miller, Van, 90
Milwaukee Bucks, 60, 108, 119–120, 122
Mitchell, Steve, 107
Moe, Doug, 80
Monroe, Earl, 37, 124, 137
Moore, Otto, 20, 41
Mullins, Jeff, 137

Nater, Swen, 95–117
   college career, 100–108
   early life, 97–100
   photos of, *94, 99, 103, 109, 113, 115*
   with San Antonio Spurs, 110–117
   with Virginia Squires, 96–97, 108–110
Nelson, Don, 53, 57, 72
New York Knicks, 37, 44, 57, 85, 87
New York Nets, 116
Nissalke, Tom, 111
North Carolina, University of, 76–79

Patterson, Steve, 33
Paultz, Billy, 114
Petrie, Geoff, 56
Pizza Hut Classic, 107
Porter, Kevin, 119, 122
Portland Trail Blazers, 55, 79

Powell, Cincy, 117
Price, Jim, 120
Purdue University, 17

Ramsay, Jack, 87
Reed, Willis, 85
Riordan, Mike, 119, 123
Rowe, Curtis, 13, 26
Russell, Bill, 22, 24, 43, 44, 53, 58, 72

St. Bonaventure University, 17, 18, 26
San Antonio Spurs, 110–117
San Diego Rockets, 49
Scott, Charlie, 80, 111
Scott, Ray, 24
Seneca High School, 128, 129, 131, 132
Shue, Gene, 135, 137, 139
Silas, Paul, 57, 72
Smith, Dean, 76
Smith, Elmore, 80, 82

Temple University, 18
Thurmond, Nate, 42, 72
Tomjanovich, Rudy, 49

UCLA (University of Southern California at Los Angeles), 77, 100–108
Unseld, Charles, 127, 147
Unseld, George, 128
Unseld, Wes, 119–147
   college career, 129–135
   early life, 127–129
   photos of, *118, 121, 126, 131, 136, 141, 145, 148*
   with Washington Bullets, 120–127, 135–147

Van Breda Kolff, Butch, 20
Van Lier, Norm, 42
Vincennes Junior College, 75, 76
Virginia Squires, 79, 96–97, 108–110, 111

Walk, Neil, 33

Walton, Bill, 100, 101, 102, 111, 116, 117
Washington Bullets, 119–127, 135–147
Westphal, Paul, 72
White, JoJo, 38, 41, 57, 74
Wooden, John, 100, 102, 104, 107
Wright, Carl, 129